Career Paths

Construction Buildings

Book 1

Virginia Evans
Jenny Dooley
Jason Revels

Express Publishing

Scope and Sequence

Unit	Topic	Reading context	Vocabulary	Function
1	Hand Tools 1	Equipment purchase request	claw hammer, flathead screwdriver, hacksaw, hand saw, level, needle nose pliers, Phillips screwdriver, slip joint pliers, tape measure, tool box, utility knife	Describing importance
2	Hand Tools 2	Advertisement	adjustable wrench, box-end wrench, chalk line reel, open-end wrench, plumb bob, sledgehammer, socket, socket wrench, speed square, snips	Making a recommendation
3	Power Tools	Magazine article	air compressor, cement mixer, circular saw, compactor, hammer drill, jackhammer, nail gun, power drill, reciprocating saw, sander	Describing uses
4	Fasteners	Website	anchor, bolt, brad, grade, metric thread, nail, nut, screw, staple, UTS thread, washer	Disagreeing with a suggestion
5	Safety Equipment	Email	dust mask, earplugs, face shield, first aid kit, goggles, grip gloves, hard hat, kneepads, leather gloves, safety glasses, steel-toe boots	Giving a warning
6	Basic Actions 1	Instruction guide	cut, drill, lift, mark, measure, nail, place, push, repeat, screw	Giving instructions
7	Basic Actions 2	Instruction guide	center, check, insert, line up, loosen, remove, slide, support, tighten, turn, twist	Giving instructions
8	Basic Math	Email	add, come to, divide by, equal, minus, multiply, plus, remainder, round up, subtract, total	Talking about amounts
9	Decimals, Fractions, and Percents	Conversion guide	convert, decimal, denominator, fraction, mixed number, numerator, percent, percentage, reduce, whole number	Correcting an error
10	Measurements	Instructions	centimeter, foot, gallon, imperial, inch, kilogram, liter, meter, metric, pound, yard	Identifying an error
11	Materials	Flyer	brick, cinder block, concrete, drywall, flooring, glass, lumber, plastic, rebar, rubber, steel	Checking information
12	Properties and Dimensions	Website	depth, dimensions, height, jamb, length, sill, strength, thickness, weight, width	Describing a change in plans
13	Site Communication	Website	communication, confirm, consult, contact, email, fax, PDF, scan, smartphone, two-way radio	Offering options
14	Parts of a Residence	Advertisement	bathroom, bedroom, garage, kitchen, living room, master bedroom, patio, roof, utility room, walk-in closet	Agreeing with an opinion
15	Parts of a Commercial Building	Email	elevator, emergency, entrance, exit, exit sign, fire escape, floor, hallway, lobby, office, stairwell	Checking items on a list

Table of Contents

flathead screwdriver

Phillips screwdriver

needle-nose pliers

slip-joint pliers

hacksaw

hand saw

Carlton Construction Co.

Equipment Purchase Request

Employee: Robert Jackson

Requested Items:

- ☑ **Phillips screwdriver**
- ☑ **flathead screwdriver**
- ☑ **claw hammer**
- ☐ tape measure
- ☐ level
- ☐ utility knife
- ☑ **needle-nose pliers**
- ☐ slip-joint pliers
- ☐ hacksaw
- ☐ hand saw
- ☑ Other: **tool box**

Reason for request: Many of my tools are missing. I need flathead and Phillips screwdrivers. I can't install doors without them. I also need a claw hammer and needle-nose pliers. I use them on every job. Finally, I need a toolbox that locks. That's because I believe that someone stole my old tools.

Get ready!

1 **Before you read the passage, talk about these questions.**

1. What are some common hand tools?
2. Which hand tool would you use to saw wood?

Reading

2 **Read the equipment purchase request. Then, mark the following statements as true (T) or false (F).**

1. __ The employee needs two types of pliers.
2. __ The employee uses a claw hammer on every job.
3. __ The employee's tool box was stolen.

Vocabulary

3 **Match the words (1-6) with the definitions (A-F).**

1. __ utility knife
2. __ flathead screwdriver
3. __ needle-nose pliers
4. __ tape measure
5. __ tool box
6. __ level

A. a tool used to turn slotted screws, which have one long slot

B. a tool used to measure how flat something is

C. hand tools with long, narrow extensions on the end, used to reach into narrow gaps

D. a portable container used to carry tools

E. a small tool used to cut various materials, such as cardboard or rope

F. a tool used to determine the length of something

4 **Fill in the blanks with the correct words and phrases from the word bank.**

WORD BANK

claw hammer   hand saw   hacksaw
Phillips screwdriver   slip-joint pliers

1. These _____ have a very firm grip.
2. Use a _____ to tighten these screws.
3. Get the _____ to remove those nails.
4. That _____ is worn from cutting so much metal.
5. A sharp _____ leaves wood with a smooth edge.

5 🎧 Listen and read the equipment purchase request again. What tools does the man use most often?

Listening

6 🎧 Listen to a conversation between a supervisor and a construction worker. Choose the correct answers.

1 What is the conversation mainly about?

    A the price of new tools

    B what tools are needed

    C how tools were lost

    D the best tools for a job

2 What is true of the woman?

    A She did not receive the purchase request

    B She wants the man to pay for new tools.

    C She does not think the tools are important.

    D She cannot do her job without new tools.

7 🎧 Listen again and complete the conversation.

Worker:	Ms. Clemmons, excuse me. Did you get my purchase request?
Supervisor:	**1** _____ , _____ . What do you need?
Worker:	Well, I need **2** _____ _____ _____ screwdrivers.
Supervisor:	Okay. Is that all?
Worker:	**3** _____ _____ . I also need a claw hammer and needle-nose pliers.
Supervisor:	That's **4** _____ _____ _____ tools. Are they that important?
Worker:	Oh, yes. I can't **5** _____ _____ _____ _____ hem.
Supervisor:	**6** _____ _____ . I'll put the order in today.

Speaking

8 With a partner, act out the roles below based on Task 7. Then, switch roles.

Student A: You are a construction worker. Talk to Student B about:

- a request for tools
- what tools are needed
- the importance of the tools

Student B: You are a supervisor. Talk to Student A about tools.

Writing

9 Use the equipment purchase request and the conversation from Task 8 to fill out the equipment request form.

Jackson Construction
Request Form

Employee: _____

Requested tools:

_____

_____

_____

Reason for request:

_____

_____

_____

box-end wrench

snips

socket wrench

open-end wrench

sledgehammer

Get ready!

1 **Before you read the passage, talk about these questions.**

1 What tool can be used to cut metal?

2 What are some different kinds of wrenches?

Reading

2 **Read the ad for a hardware store. Then, mark the statements as true (T) or false (F).**

1 __ Box-end and open-end wrenches are available together in a set.

2 __ The socket wrench set does not include sockets.

3 __ Chalk line reels are marking tools.

Vocabulary

3 **Match the words (1-5) with the definitions (A-E).**

1 __ plumb bob   4 __ chalk line reel

2 __ speed square   5 __ socket

3 __ snips

A strong scissors used to cut sheet metal or similar materials

B a triangle-shaped tool used to draw straight lines and angles

C a head that attaches to a wrench for tightening different sized bolts

D a weight attached to a line used to determine if something is perpendicular to something else

E a tool that leaves a straight line on a flat surface

4 **Read the sentences and choose the correct words or phrases.**

1 I have several heads for this **adjustable wrench / socket wrench**.

2 Put the end of the **box-end wrench / open-end wrench** completely around the bolt.

3 Are you strong enough to lift that **socket wrench / sledgehammer**?

4 A(n) **box-end wrench / open-end wrench** only grasps opposite sides of a bolt.

5 Make the opening of that **adjustable wrench / socket wrench** smaller to fit the bolt.

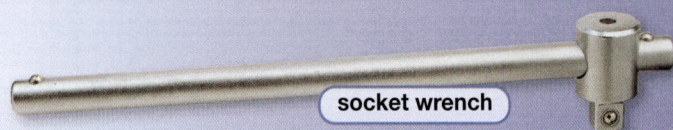

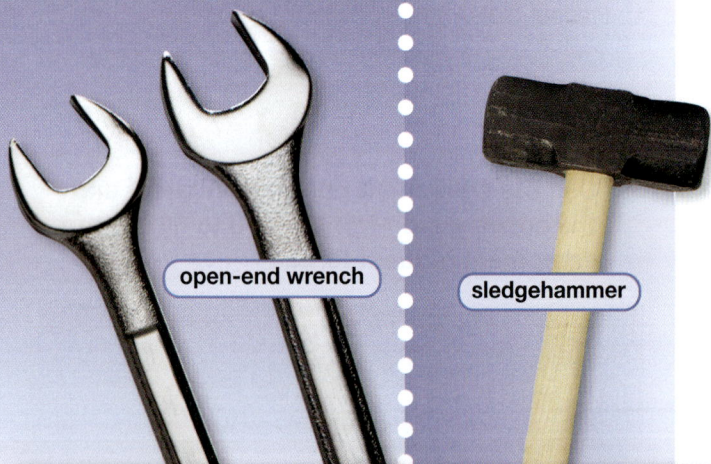

JOHN'S HARDWARE
SPECIAL SALE!

John's Hardware is having a special sale on hand tools! From **sledgehammers** to **snips**, everything is available at a low price! Here are some of the great deals.

Adjustable wrenches are on sale for just $7.00. We also have sets of five **box-end wrenches** or **open-end wrenches** for $16.00 each. The deluxe **socket wrench** set comes with eight **sockets**. It's only $28.00 this week!

But that's not all. Our accurate measuring and marking tools are on sale, too. **Speed squares** are only $4.00 each. **Plumb bobs** and **chalk line reels** are available for just $8.00.

5 🎧 **Listen and read the ad for a hardware store again. What types of marking tools does the store have?**

Listening

6 🎧 **Listen to a conversation between a customer and a clerk. Choose the correct answers.**

1   What is the conversation mainly about?
   A   buying individual tools or a set
   B   listing the sizes wrenches come in
   C   finding the right size of wrench for a job
   D   explaining differences between wrench types

2   What will the man likely do next?
   A   search for sockets
   B   buy the wrench set
   C   compare wrench sizes
   D   return his socket wrench

7 🎧 **Listen again and complete the conversation.**

Clerk:	Hello, Sir. How may I help you?
Customer:	I'm **1** _____ _____ a socket wrench.
Clerk:	Sure. Do you need **2** _____ , too?
Customer:	Probably **3** _____ _____ . What do you have?
Clerk:	Well, you can buy a wrench for eight dollars. The sockets **4** _____ _____ three dollars each.
Customer:	I see. That sounds expensive.
Clerk:	**5** _____ _____ _____ the socket wrench set. It comes with eight sockets. And it's just twenty dollars this week.
Customer:	Perfect. **6** _____ _____ the set.

Speaking

8 **With a partner, act out the roles below based on Task 7. Then, switch roles.**

USE LANGUAGE SUCH AS:

I'm looking for ...
That sounds ...
Then I recommend ...

Student A: You are a store clerk. Talk to Student B about:
 • what he or she needs
 • tool options
 • what you recommend

Student B: You are a customer. Talk to Student A about which product you should buy.

Writing

9 **Use the ad and the conversation from Task 8 to fill out the invoice.**

JOHN'S HARDWARE
Invoice

Product(s) purchased:	Cost:
_____	_____
_____	_____

3 Power Tools

compressor

The Handy Man Magazine Guide to Power Tools

By Marcus Ericson

Do you want high quality power tools? Here are the best toolmakers around.

Every toolbox needs a drill or two! For a **hammer drill** or **power drill**, try Bentley Tools. Their drills and **nail guns** are reliable and powerful. And Bentley tools are cordless. Take them anywhere!

For a **circular** or **reciprocating saw**, Cutco won't let you down. You get a smooth, accurate cut every time.

Do you need a **sander**? Try Sandman Tools. Their sanders smooth all woods and metals.

Marshall Industries makes great **air compressors** and **cement mixers**.

Finally, heavy-duty materials need heavy-duty tools. Builder's Source **jackhammers** cut through rock and pavement easily! This company also makes **compactors**. They flatten any type of soil.

jackhammer

cement mixer

circular saw

power drill

Get ready!

① Before you read the passage, talk about these questions.

1 What are some common power tools that construction workers use?

2 What machine makes cement?

Reading

② Read the article from *Handy Man* magazine. Then, mark the statements as true (T) or false (F).

1 ___ Bentley Tools makes multiple types of drills.

2 ___ The author recommends Sandman Tools for all saws.

3 ___ Builder's Source makes tools to flatten the ground.

Vocabulary

③ Write a word that is similar in meaning to the underlined part.

1 To cut through the wood, use a <u>device with a rotating metal disk that has sharp teeth</u>.
_ i _ _ _ l _ r   _ _ w

2 Joe's <u>tool that breaks up hard surfaces</u> is broken.
_ _ c k _ _ _ m _ _

3 Start laying concrete after the <u>rotating barrel</u> mixes everything.
_ _ _ e _ t   _ _ x _ _

4 Get the <u>electrically powered tool with a rotating bit</u>.
_ o _ _ r   _ _ _ _ l

5 Before you paint the wood, use a <u>machine that makes wood smooth</u> on it.
_ _ n _ e _

6 If the wall is too hard to hammer the nail into it, try the <u>device that drives nails into a surface when you pull a trigger</u>.
_ _ i _   _ u _

4 Read the sentences and choose the correct words or phrases.

1 The **reciprocating saw / circular saw** cuts through materials by going back and forth.

2 To make a hole in the stone, use a **nail gun / hammer drill**.

3 Use the **cement mixer / compactor** to flatten the ground.

4 Since there's no electricity in here, hook up the jackhammer to the **air compressor / sander**.

5 🎧 **Listen and read the article from *Handy Man* magazine again. What are the benefits of a Bentley Tools power drill?**

Listening

6 🎧 **Listen to a conversation between two construction workers. Check (✓) the benefits of the new tool.**

1 ❏ costs little money
2 ❏ long-lasting battery
3 ❏ drills through concrete
4 ❏ drills through steel
5 ❏ has extra batteries

7 🎧 **Listen again and complete the conversation.**

Worker 1: Kyle, is that **1** _____ _____ _____ Bentley power drills?

Worker 2: Yes. It's the Power Drill 3000.

Worker 1: Aren't they **2** _____ ?

Worker 2: Yes, but it's **3** _____ _____ _____ . It drills into everything. Wood, concrete, steel, everything.

Worker 1: Wow! It's cordless, right? Does the battery **4** _____ _____ ?

Worker 2: Unfortunately, no. But it's not a **5** _____ _____ .

Worker 1: How so?

Worker 2: It came with extra batteries. So if it **6** _____ _____ , I just put in another.

Speaking

8 With a partner, act out the roles below based on Task 7. Then, switch roles.

USE LANGUAGE SUCH AS:

Is that one of those ...?
Aren't they ...?
Wow! It's ..., right?

Student A: You are a construction worker. Talk to Student B about:
• a new power tool
• its cost
• its benefits

Student B: You are a construction worker. Talk to Student A about a new power tool.

Writing

9 Use the article and the conversation from Task 8 to fill out an online review.

Tool Central

Please rate your recent power tool purchase

User name: _____

Date of purchase: _____

Item purchased: _____

Star rating (1 star = terrible; 5 stars = great):

What did you think of it? Write a short review:

_____
_____
_____
_____

HOME   ABOUT US   SERVICES   CONTACT

screws

nails

bolt and nut

washer

anchors

staples

Barnes Fasteners

Know the Right Fastener for Your Task

Sometimes you need more than a simple **screw** or **nail**. More complex tasks require more complex fasteners. Here are some suggestions.

Fasten structural wood-to-wood connections with heavy **bolts**. Always use a **washer** to reduce pressure. Bolts without tapered ends should be secured with a **nut**. **Anchors** hold screws or bolts in weak materials.

There's more to know about bolts, though. Know what **grade** to buy. And check if you need **UTS thread** or **metric thread**.

Smaller fasteners are equally useful. **Brads** are great for hanging pictures or other household tasks. And **staples** are not just for paper! For example, large ones attach shingles to a roof.

Get ready!

① **Before you read the passage, talk about these questions.**

1 What are some different types of fasteners?

2 A screwdriver is used to insert what fastener?

Reading

② **Read the website for a fastener manufacturer. Then, mark the statements as true (T) or false (F).**

1 __ Heavy bolts can make structural connections.

2 __ Nuts should be used to secure an anchor.

3 __ Shingles are attached to roofs with brads.

Vocabulary

③ **Match the words (1-5) with the definitions (A-E).**

1__ screw   4 __ brad

2__ washer   5 __ bolt

3__ staple

A a thin, small nail with a slight projection at the top on one side

B a metal fastener with a threaded body and held in place with a nut on the end opposite the head

C a flat disk placed beneath a nut to distribute pressure or prevent leaking

D a metal fastener with a threaded shank that is driven into place with a screwdriver

E a U-shaped fastener used to hold something together by penetrating it and curling around it

④ **Read the sentence pairs. Choose which word or phrase best fits each blank.**

1 grade / anchor

  A Use a(n) _____ if the material is too weak to hold the screw.

  B Can you tell me the _____ of that bolt?

2 metric thread / UTS thread

  A _____ measures a screw's thread in millimeters.

  B _____ is most commonly used in the United States.

3 nut / nail

  A Don't forget to secure the bolt with a _____ .

  B This hammer is too small to drive this _____ .

5 🎧 **Listen and read the website for a fastener manufacturer again. What jobs are different fasteners used for?**

Listening

6 🎧 **Listen to a conversation between two construction workers. Choose the correct answers.**

1   What problem do the workers discuss?

   A   They need small bolts.

   B   They need different grade bolts.

   C   They cannot find the right size nuts.

   D   They used the wrong size bolts.

2   What will the woman likely do next?

   A   return to the tool shed

   B   take the man's bolts

   C   purchase new bolts

   D   attach the beams

7 🎧 **Listen again and complete the conversation.**

Worker 1:	Joe, do you have any grade five bolts **1** _____ _____ ?
Worker 2:	Um, no. Why do you ask?
Worker 1:	I'm attaching structural wood beams. I **2** _____ _____ _____ bolts.
Worker 2:	Well, I do have some grade two bolts. **3** _____ _____ _____ use those?
Worker 1:	Thanks, but there's **4** _____ _____ I can use them.
Worker 2:	Really? **5** _____ _____ ?
Worker 1:	They're too weak. They can't support **6** _____ _____ _____ a grade five bolt.
Worker 2:	I see. So what's your plan?
Worker 1:	I'll head back to the tool shed. We have plenty of bolts there.

Speaking

8 **With a partner, act out the roles below based on Task 7. Then, switch roles.**

Student A: You are a construction worker. Talk to Student B about:

•   what type of fastener you need

•   why another fastener won't work

•   what you should do

Student B: You are a construction worker. Talk to Student A about what type of fastener they need.

Writing

9 **Use the website and the conversation from Task 8 to fill out the supply sheet.**

Jackson Construction

Supply Sheet

List each item you take, the number, and what job they are needed for.

Items needed: _____

_____

_____

Amount taken: _____

_____

_____

Needed for: _____

_____

_____

face shield

earplugs

steel-toe boots

goggles

dust mask

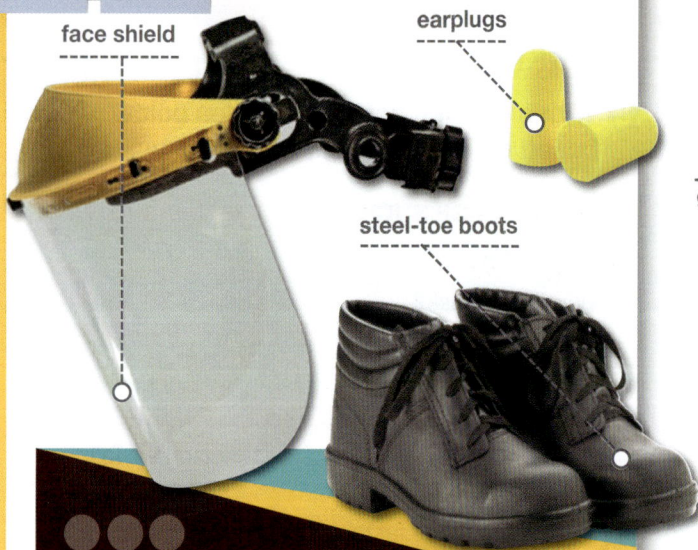

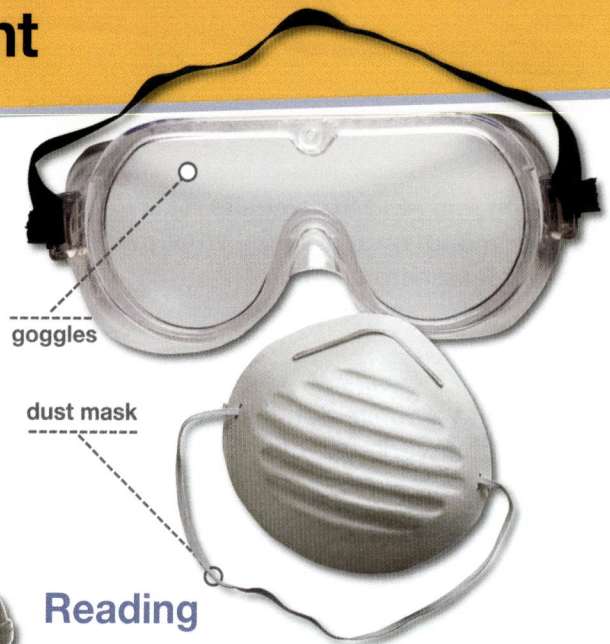

To: r.ortiz@desertconstruction.com,
t.jacobs@desertconstruction.com,
p.alfonso@desertconstruction.com
From: t.klein@desertconstruction.com
Subject: Safety Equipment

Dear Site Managers,

Last week, an employee was injured. A cement block fell and broke his toes. We want to avoid these injuries.

Remind all employees to wear personal protective equipment (PPE). To enter the construction site, everyone needs **steel-toe boots**, **hard hats**, and **safety glasses** or **goggles**. Employees need to wear **leather gloves** when nailing, doing electrical work, and sanding or cutting wood. **Dust masks** or **face shields** are also essential for wood cutting. **Earplugs** are necessary when working with loud tools like jackhammers. Anyone handling a power tool must also wear **grip gloves**. **Kneepads** must be worn when working on the ground.

Finally, keep **first aid kits** on site. Make sure everyone knows where they are. If we follow these guidelines, injuries won't be a problem.

Thanks,
Tim Klein
Owner, Desert Construction

Get ready!

① **Before you read the passage, talk about these questions.**

1   What is some safety equipment used on a construction site?

2   What safety equipment protects a worker's feet?

Reading

② **Read the email on safety equipment. Then, complete the table using information from the email.**

Situation	PPE needed
Arriving at the construction site	_____
Working with wood	_____
Using loud power tools	_____

Vocabulary

③ **Write a word or phrase that is similar in meaning to the underlined part.**

1   Wear a <u>partial face covering that protects your mouth and nose</u> when you sand wood.
_ _ _ t   m _ _ _

2   When installing floors, wear <u>equipment that protects the knees</u>.   _ _ _ _ p _ d s

3   John wore <u>small pieces of plastic</u> so that the noise from the machinery didn't hurt his ears.
_ _ r p _ _ _ _

4   To avoid head injuries from falling objects, wear a <u>helmet made of plastic or metal.</u>
_ _ r _   _ _ t

5   Greg wasn't hurt when he dropped the wood because he was wearing <u>shoes that have extra reinforcement at the toes</u>.
_ _ _ _ l - _ o _   _ _ _ t s

6   Using some chemicals or tools requires a <u>protective covering for your entire face</u>.
_ a _ _   _ h _ _ _ d

7   <u>Protective eyewear that shields the eyes and area around them</u> are necessary when drilling.
_ _ _ _ l _ s

④ Match the words (1-4) with the definitions (A-D).

1 __ first aid kit   3 __ safety glasses
2 __ grip gloves   4 __ leather gloves

A safety equipment that protects the hands
B a container that has items needed to treat a small injury
C protective eyewear that uses shatterproof glass
D protective equipment that helps people to hold things firmly

⑤ 🎧 Listen and read the email on safety equipment again. What do you think is the most important piece of safety equipment? Why?

Listening

⑥ 🎧 Listen to a conversation between a manager and a construction worker. Mark the following statements as true (T) or false (F).

1 __ The man is not wearing his safety equipment.
2 __ The company was fined by an inspector.
3 __ The man received a written warning.

⑦ 🎧 Listen again and complete the conversation.

Manager:	Richard, where are your hard hat and safety glasses?
Worker:	I just 1 _____ _____ _____ .
Manager:	Well, you need to wear them 2 _____ _____ _____ . Otherwise, the safety inspectors can fine us.
Worker:	I'm sorry. It's just that it's so hot 3 _____ _____ !
Manager:	I know it is. But you could be hurt or killed 4 _____ _____ .
Worker:	Okay. I'll put them 5 _____ _____ .
Manager:	Thank you. This is just a verbal warning. 6 _____ _____ , it'll be a written warning.
Worker:	I understand!

Speaking

⑧ With a partner, act out the roles below based on Task 7. Then, switch roles.

USE LANGUAGE SUCH AS:

Where are your ...?
You need to wear ...
Next time ...

Student A: You are a construction site manager. Talk to Student B about:
• a piece of safety equipment
• why the person needs to wear it
• the consequences of not wearing it

Student B: You are a construction worker. Talk to Student A about proper personal protective equipment.

Writing

⑨ Use the email and the conversation from Task 8 to fill out the written warning.

Written Warning

Employee name: _____
Date of incident: _____

Reason for warning: _____
_____
_____

Actions Taken: _____
_____
_____

measure

drill

How to Raise a Stud Wall

1 Choose the location for the new wall. **Mark** that spot on the ceiling.

2 **Cut** the top plate and **screw** it into place.

3 Mark where the base plate will go.

4 **Measure** and cut the base plate.

5 Measure and cut the studs.

6 **Place** the completed studs into position.

7 **Nail** two spikes into the base of a stud. **Repeat** this for each stud.

8 **Lift** the new wall frame and **push** it into place. Nail it to the top plate.

9 **Drill** holes for wires or pipes if needed.

screw

nail

Reading

2 Read the instruction guide on raising a wall. Then, mark the statements as true (T) or false (F).

1 __ The base plate is cut before the top plate.

2 __ Two spikes are nailed into each stud.

3 __ Holes should be drilled in studs before they are nailed in place.

Vocabulary

3 Match the words (1-5) with the definitions (A-E).

1 __ lift   3 __ push   5 __ cut

2 __ mark   4 __ place

A to set something somewhere

B to divide something with a sharp instrument

C to write a sign on something for reference

D to apply force to something so that it moves away

E to pick something up

Get ready!

1 Before you read the passage, talk about these questions.

1 What are some basic actions done when building?

2 What action involves putting a hole in something?

4 Read the sentences and choose the correct words.

1 Can you **measure / drill** one meter of this board?
2 **Lift / Repeat** the same actions to install each window.
3 **Cut / Nail** these two boards together.
4 Please **drill / push** a hole in this wall.
5 Do not **place / screw** the fixture into the wall yet.

5 🎧 Listen and read the instruction guide on raising a wall again. What are some steps to raising a wall?

Listening

6 🎧 Listen to a conversation between two construction workers. Choose the correct answers.

1 What is the conversation mainly about?
   A drilling holes   C finishing a wall
   B cutting studs   D measuring a frame

2 What will the man likely do next?
   A get some nails
   B lift the wall frame up
   C hold the frame in place
   D nail the frame to the top plate

7 🎧 Listen again and complete the conversation.

Worker 1:	Sally, could you help me **1** _____ _____ _____ ?
Worker 2:	Sure, Phil. What **2** _____ _____ _____ ?
Worker 1:	I'm finishing this wall. Please help me **3** _____ _____ _____ into place.
Worker 2:	**4** _____ _____ .
Worker 1:	Great. Now, please **5** _____ _____ _____ in place. I'll nail it to the top plate.
Worker 2:	Okay. Do you need some nails?
Worker 1:	**6** _____ _____ _____ in my pocket.
Worker 2:	Just checking. I have the frame. Go ahead and nail it.

Speaking

8 With a partner, act out the roles below based on Task 7. Then, switch roles.

USE LANGUAGE SUCH AS:

Please help me ...
Now, please ...
Do you need ...?

Student A: You are a construction worker Talk to Student B about:
• help with a task
• what you need Student B to do
• what supplies you have or need

Student B: You are a construction worker. Talk to Student A about a task.

Writing

9 Use the introduction guide and the conversation from Task 8 to fill out the note.

Note

Mr. Jackson,
The wall is almost finished. I _____
and _____ the studs. The top plate is
_____ to the ceiling. I just need someone
to help me _____ the frame. Then I will
_____ the frame to the top plate.

remove

support

loosen

insert

tighten

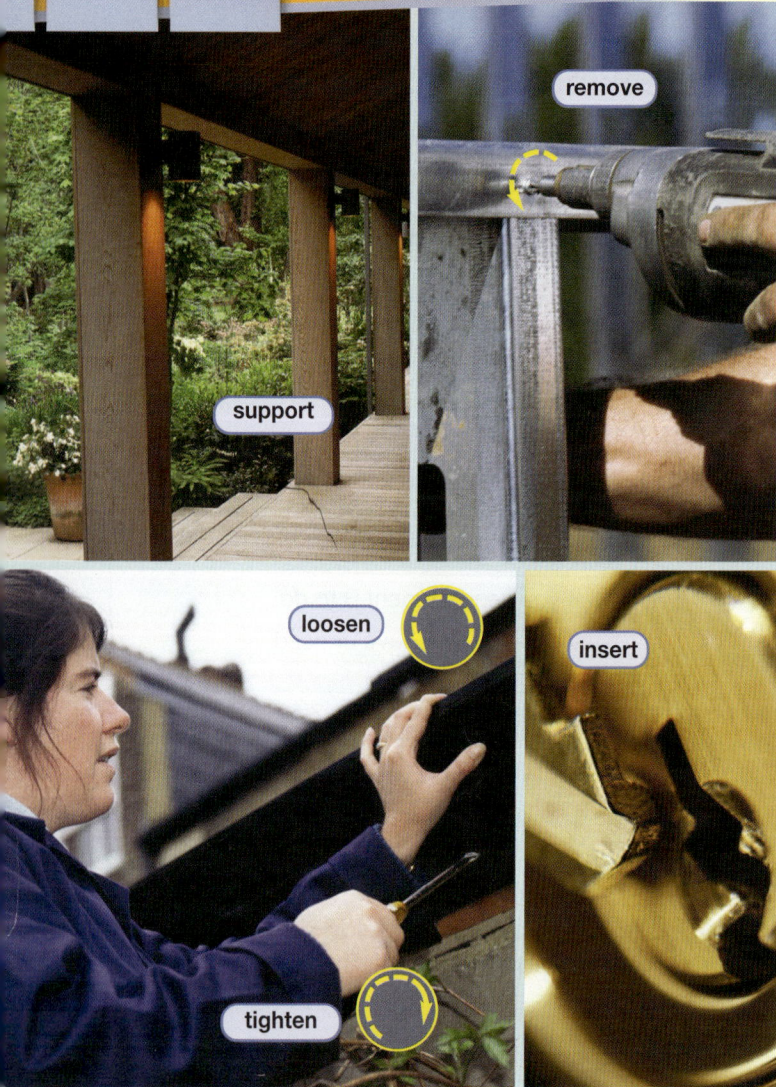

New Door Installation

To install a new door in your home, follow these simple steps:

1 **Check** the door opening. Make sure the sides are plumb.

2 Lift the door into the opening and **slide** it into place.

3 **Support** the door with boards or have another person hold it. **Line up** the door to the hinges.

4 Attach the door to the hinges. **Turn** the screws until they are against the hinges.

5 Open and close the door. If it does not swing freely, **loosen** the screws. But do not **remove** them. Insert shims to **center** the door and **tighten** the screws.

6 **Insert** the doorknob. Tighten the screws until they are secure.

7 **Twist** the doorknob to make sure it operates correctly.

Get ready!

❶ **Before you read the passage, talk about these questions.**

1 What actions are done when using a screwdriver?

2 What is another word for taking a screw out?

Reading

❷ **Read the guide to installing a door. Then, mark the statements as true (T) or false (F).**

1 __ The doorknob is inserted before the door is put in place.

2 __ The installation requires two people.

3 __ Shims should be inserted if the door does not open and close correctly.

Vocabulary

❸ **Match the words (1-6) with the definitions (A-F).**

1 __ support   4 __ insert

2 __ slide   5 __ turn

3 __ remove   6 __ twist

A to push something horizontally

B to keep something from falling down

C to change something's direction

D to take something out of something else

E to cause something to rotate

F to put something inside something else

❹ **Fill in the blanks with the correct words and phrases from the word bank.**

word BANK

loosen   center

check   tighten   line up

1 Please _____ that picture between the two others.

2 You should _____ that screw more before it falls out.

3 Could you _____ to see if that is the right length?

4 Turn screws left to _____ them.

5 Make sure the two ends of the pipe _____ correctly.

5 🎧 **Listen and read the guide to installing a door again. What should people do if a door does not open and close correctly?**

Listening

6 🎧 **Listen to a conversation between two construction workers. Choose the correct answers.**

1 What is the conversation mainly about?

    A installing a new doorknob

    B repairing a door installation

    C testing a door installation

    D listing steps of an installation

2 What will the woman likely do next?

    A test the door

    B remove the screws

    C center the plate

    D support the door

7 🎧 **Listen again and complete the conversation.**

Worker 1: Hey, Brenda, did you install this door?

Worker 2: Yes, I did. Is **1** _____ _____ ?

Worker 1: It's not closing properly.

Worker 2: Oh, I'm sorry about that. What should I do **2** _____ _____ _____ ?

Worker 1: First, **3** _____ _____ _____ on the bottom hinge. Then insert a shim and tighten the screws again.

Worker 2: Okay. I'll do that **4** _____ _____ . But can you give me a hand?

Worker 1: **5** _____ . What do you need?

Worker 2: I'll need you to **6** _____ _____ _____ while I insert the shim.

Speaking

8 **With a partner, act out the roles below based on Task 7. Then, switch roles.**

> **USE LANGUAGE SUCH AS:**
>
> *Did you ...?*
>
> *First, ...*
>
> *Can you give me a hand?*

Student A: You are a construction worker. Talk to Student B about:

- a problem with a door
- what is wrong with the door
- how to fix the problem

Student B: You are a construction worker. Talk to Student A about a problem with the door.

Writing

9 **Use the guide and the conversation from Task 8 to fill out the construction worker's notes.**

Door Installation

Problem: _____

_____

_____

_____

Solution: _____

_____

_____

_____

8 Basic Math

"6.759 = 7.0"

round up

come to

X multiply

+ add

— subtract

÷ divide

To: Charles Gordon
From: Barbara Welch
Re: Cost of Materials Order

Charles,

You asked why the order was so expensive. We need about two and a half bags of concrete for each structure. I **rounded up** to three bags per structure. There are ten structures. When you **multiply** that, it **equals** thirty bags. That part of the order was $150. The cost of concrete **plus** the cost of rebar **came to** over $600. When you **add** shipping costs, it **totals** $650.

I can **subtract** a few items to save money. The total **minus** the cost of rebar is around $175. Or, we can make several payments. The bill **divided by** three payments is about $215. We could pay the **remainder** with the last payment. Let me know what you prefer.

Barbara

Get ready!

❶ **Before you read the passage, talk about these questions.**

1 What calculations increase a total number?
2 What calculations decrease a total number?

Reading

❷ **Read the email about the cost of materials. Then, mark the statements as true (T) or false (F).**

1 __ The company is working on thirty structures.
2 __ The cost of rebar was more expensive than the cost of concrete.
3 __ Shipping costs were about $175.

Vocabulary

❸ **Match the words (1-5) with the definitions (A-E).**

1 __ subtract   4 __ round up
2 __ multiply   5 __ divide
3 __ add

A to increase a number to a greater whole number, often ending in zero
B to split a number into equal amounts
C to take one number away from another
D to combine two or more numbers
E to add one number to itself a specific number of times

4 **Read the sentences and choose the correct words.**

1 The charges together **plus / come to** $35.50.

2 Twelve **minus / plus** five equals 17.

3 What is the **remainder / multiply** when you divide 16 by 3?

4 Nineteen **add / minus** four is fifteen.

5 Ten minus two **equals / rounds up** six plus two.

5 🎧 **Listen and read the email about the cost of materials again. What are some ways to describe a total amount after items are added together?**

Listening

6 🎧 **Listen to a conversation between a clerk and a construction company manager. Choose the correct answers.**

1 What is the conversation mainly about?

A rounding up a total

B adding items to an order

C subtracting shipping costs

D dividing payments for an order

2 What is true of the total?

A The woman wants to divide it.

B The man added to it incorrectly.

C It is lower after subtracting items.

D It does not include shipping costs.

7 🎧 **Listen again and complete the conversation.**

Clerk: Okay, Ms. Hoffman, I'll **1** _____ _____ your invoice. What can I do for you?

Manager: I have to **2** _____ _____ _____ of my order.

Clerk: Sure. **3** _____ _____ _____ beams do you need?

Manager: I want to **4** _____ _____ to the original fifteen.

Clerk: So fifteen **5** _____ five is twenty. Your new total **6** _____ _____ $976.12.

Speaking

8 **With a partner, act out the roles below based on Task 7. Then, switch roles.**

USE LANGUAGE SUCH AS:

What can I do ...?

I'd like to ...

Your new total ...

Student A: You are a clerk. Talk to Student B about:

- a change to an order
- what kind of change is needed
- the new total for the order

Student B: You are a construction company manager. Talk to Student A about a change to an order.

Writing

9 **Use the email and the conversation from Task 8 to fill out the invoice.**

Gibbs Building Supply

Confirmation of Changes

Customer: _____

Item: _____

Original order: _____

New order: _____

New cost: _____

Explanation of changes: _____

_____

_____

Decimals, Fractions, and Percents

7/8

numerator

7/8

denominator

75%

percent

2/3

fraction

0.26

decimal

1 3/8

mixed number

The Construction Assistant:

Converting Decimals, Fractions, and Percents

1 **Reducing** Fractions: Divide the **numerator** and **denominator** by the same number. Repeat if necessary until both cannot be divided into **whole numbers**.

2 **Percentages**: A **percent** is a fraction. Its denominator is 100. So 71% is equal to 71/100. In **decimal** form, this is 0.71.

It is usually easier to do calculations with decimals instead of **fractions**. Convert measurements that are fractions to decimal form.

3 **Convert** a fraction to a decimal: Divide the numerator by the denominator.

4 Convert a **mixed number** to a decimal: First, write the whole number. Place a decimal point to its right. Change the fraction to a decimal (see above). Then, write it to the right of the decimal point.

Get ready!

1 Before you read the passage, talk about these questions.

1 What are some ways of showing numbers that are not whole?

2 What is ½ displayed as a percent?

Reading

2 Read the guide about converting fractions, decimals, and percents. Then, mark the statements as true (T) or false (F).

1 ___ Divide the numerator and the denominator to reduce a fraction.

2 ___ The denominator of any percent is 100.

3 ___ Divide the denominator by the numerator to convert a fraction to a decimal.

Vocabulary

3 Match the words (1-5) with the definitions (A-E).

1 ___ numerator   4 ___ whole number

2 ___ fraction   5 ___ denominator

3 ___ percent

A a number that is not divided into parts

B the lower number of a fraction

C a ratio of two numbers, expressed with one number written above the other

D the upper number of a fraction

E a number that expresses a part of something per hundred

4 Fill in the blanks with the correct words and phrases from the word bank.

WORD BANK

decimal   convert   percentage
reduce   mixed number

1 The expression 12 $\frac{2}{3}$ is a _____ .

2 _____ that fraction to its simplest terms.

3 What _____ of the insulation is installed?

4 Please _____ that fraction to a decimal.

5 _____ numbers are usually more accurate than fractions.

5 🎧 Listen and read the guide about converting fractions, decimals, and percents again. How do you convert a fraction into a decimal?

Listening

6 🎧 Listen to a conversation between a construction worker and a manager. Choose the correct answers.

1 What is the conversation mainly about?

   A reducing a fraction

   B working with mixed numbers

   C comparing decimals and fractions

   D converting a fraction to a decimal

2 How should the man write the result?

   A as a whole number

   B as a decimal

   C as a mixed number

   D as a percent

7 🎧 Listen again and complete the conversation.

Worker:	I **1** _____ _____ _____ this. How do you convert a fraction to a decimal?
Manager:	Ah, where are you **2** _____ _____ ?
Worker:	Well, you **3** _____ _____ _____ by the numerator, right?
Manager:	No, you divide **4** _____ _____ by the denominator.
Worker:	Oh, I see. That makes a lot **5** _____ _____ . Thanks for the help.
Manager:	You're welcome. I **6** _____ _____ with those, too.

Speaking

8 With a partner, act out the roles below based on Task 7. Then, switch roles.

Student A: You are a construction worker. Talk to Student B about:

• doing a conversion calculation

• correcting a mistake

Student B: You are a manager. Talk to Student A about doing a conversion calculation.

Writing

9 Use the guide and the conversation from Task 8 to complete the email.

●●●
Converting fractions

Hi _____ ,

You made a mistake on your conversion. You

_____ _____ .

But you're supposed to _____ .

Please remember this for next time. Thanks,

_____

Instructions for mixing cement

Concrete mixing follows a 1:2:3 mix: 1 part Portland cement, 2 parts sand, and 3 parts aggregate. However, should you desire exact measurements, use the following amounts.

Concrete Mixing Instructions (Imperial)

Ingredients:
- One 94 **pound** bag of Portland cement
- 15 **gallons** of sand
- 22 gallons of gravel

Mix the dry ingredients. Then add water in small amounts. One bag will produce about six square **yards** of cement. The average layer thickness is 4 **inches**. That's 1/3 of a **foot**.

Concrete Mixing Instructions (Metric)

Ingredients:
- One 43 **kilogram** bag of Portland cement
- 57 **liters** of sand
- 83 liters of gravel

Mix the dry ingredients. Then add water in small amounts. One bag will produce about five square **meters** of cement. The average layer thickness is 10 **centimeters**.

1 in. = 2.54 cm

1 cm = 0.3937 in.

1 yard = 0.9144 m

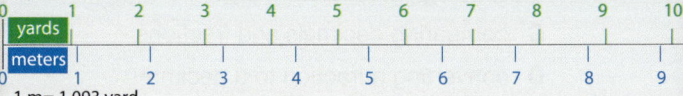

1 m= 1.093 yard

1 pound = 0.453 kilos

1 kilo = 2.205 pounds

IMPERIAL UNITS
METRIC UNITS

Get ready!

1 Before you read the passage, talk about these questions.

1 What are some imperial units of measurements?
2 What are some metric units of measurement?

Reading

2 Read the instructions for mixing cement. Then, mark the statements as true (T) or false (F).

1 ___ Forty pounds of cement is equal to 60 kilos.
2 ___ Water should be added after the sand and cement are mixed.
3 ___ One bag of cement will produce a layer with thickness of 5 inches or 2 centimeters.

Vocabulary

3 Match the words (1-6) with the definitions (A-F).

1 ___ liter   4 ___ inch
2 ___ pound   5 ___ gallon
3 ___ kilogram   6 ___ meter

A a metric unit of mass
B a metric unit of volume
C an imperial unit of length
D an imperial unit of mass
E a metric unit of length
F an imperial unit of volume

4 Read the sentences and choose the correct words.

1 The yard and the gallon are **metric / imperial** units of measurement.
2 Lay out ten **yards / centimeters** of cement between the building and the street.
3 The board is only five **kilograms / feet** long.
4 The bolt is about eight **centimeters / gallons** long.
5 The meter and kilogram are **metric / imperial** units of measurement.

⑤ 🎧 Listen and read the instructions for mixing cement again. What way is the concrete mixed?

Listening

⑥ 🎧 Listen to a conversation between two construction workers. Choose the correct answers.

1   What is the conversation mainly about?

   A   how to make concrete harder

   B   which solid and liquid ingredients are needed

   C   differences between imperial and metric measurements

   D   why the concrete mix is not working

2   What will the woman likely do next?

   A   get more solid ingredients

   B   mix the concrete again

   C   convert the liquid ingredients to imperial units

   D   change the dry ingredients to metric units

⑦ 🎧 Listen again and complete the conversation.

Worker 1:	This concrete mix is not turning out right. I can't **1** _____ _____ what's wrong.
Worker 2:	Did you use the 1:2:3 mix?
Worker 1:	No, I used specific measurements.
Worker 2:	Hmm, let me check your measurements. Oh, I see **2** _____ _____.
Worker 1:	Did I **3** _____ _____ _____ ?
Worker 2:	Yeah, you used imperial units for the liquid ingredients. Then you used **4** _____ _____ for the dry ones.
Worker 1:	Oh, my. Well, that will cause **5** _____ _____ . I'll be sure to use all metric. I'll go make a new batch.
Worker 2:	Glad I **6** _____ _____ .

Speaking

⑧ With a partner, act out the roles below based on Task 7. Then, switch roles.

USE LANGUAGE SUCH AS:

I can't figure out ...

Let me take a look ...

You used ...

Student A: You are a construction worker. Talk to Student B about:

•   a problem with a concrete mix

•   a mistake with measurements

•   how to fix the mistake

Student B: You are a construction worker. Talk to Student A about a problem with a concrete mix.

Writing

⑨ Use the instructions and the conversation from Task 8 to fill out the measurement chart.

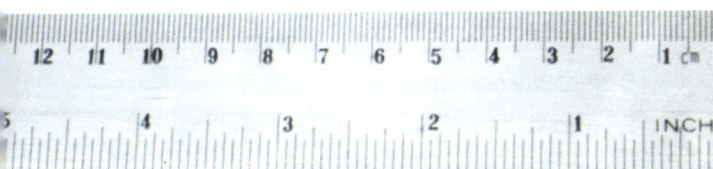

measurement chart

	Metric units	Imperial units
Length		
Weight		
Volume		

23

steel rebar

bricks

cinder blocks

drywall

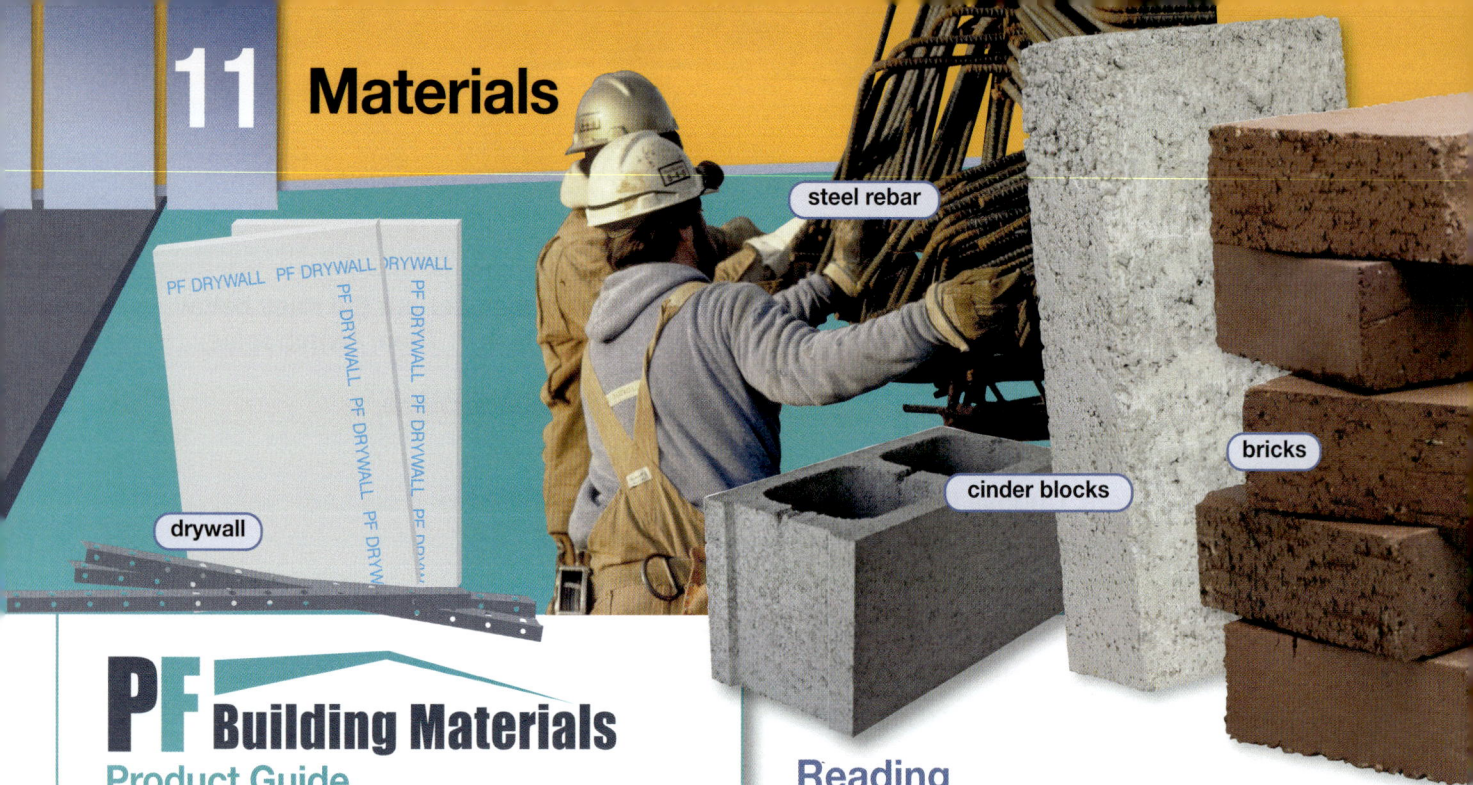

PF Building Materials

Product Guide

PF Building Materials has a product for every building need.

Concrete: We sell cement in 40 kilogram bags for mixing. We also have pre-made **cinder blocks** for load-bearing walls.

Steel: Steel **rebars** are available in two meter segments.

Lumber: Lumber is available in all standard dimensions.

Drywall: Drywall is the ideal material for walls of new rooms. Panels are 120 cm wide.

Bricks: We have a variety of decorative bricks for exterior walls and walkways. They are sold individually or by the pallet.

Glass: Sheets of glass for windows and doors can be cut to any size.

Flooring: We have a wide selection of flooring tiles available. They are made from **plastic**, **rubber**, stone, and other materials.

rubber

Get ready!

1 Before you read the passage, talk about these questions.

1 What are some different building materials?

2 What material can be used to reinforce a concrete structure?

Reading

2 Read the flyer for a materials supplier. Then, choose the correct answers.

1 What is the main idea of the article?

  A the strongest building materials

  B which materials a supplier offers

  C types of materials to use in walls

  D ways to reduce building materials costs

2 How is drywall sold?

  A in any size   **C** in 2 meter segments

  B by the pallet   **D** in 120 cm wide panels

3 Which of the following is NOT a material for flooring tiles?

  A stone   **C** plastic

  B rubber   **D** glass

Vocabulary

3 Match the words (1-5) with the definitions (A-E).

1 __ concrete   4 __ brick

2 __ glass   5 __ lumber

3 __ flooring

A a building material made of rectangular blocks of hardened clay

B a mix of cement, water, gravel, and sand used as a building material

C processed wood used as a building material

D material used in floors

E a solid, breakable, and transparent material often used to make windows

4 Read the sentence pairs. Choose which word or phrase best fits each blank.

1 rebars / cinder blocks

   A There are several _____ running through this concrete wall to support it.

   B Stack those _____ to form a wall.

2 plastic / drywall

   A These bathroom floor tiles are made of _____ .

   B Install _____ in the new room.

3 rubber / steel

   A _____ bars give this building a very solid frame.

   B The contractor will install a _____ floor in this gym.

5 🎧 Listen and read the flyer for a materials supplier again. What materials can be used in floors?

Listening

6 🎧 Listen to a conversation between a clerk and a customer. Mark the following statements as true (T) or false (F).

1 __ The woman is adding a porch to her front yard.

2 __ The company sells lumber by the yard.

3 __ The woman needs a pallet of bricks.

7 🎧 Listen again and complete the conversation.

Customer:	Hello. I'd like to **1** _____ _____ _____ for some lumber and brick. I'm adding a deck to my backyard.
Clerk:	Certainly. What **2** _____ _____ _____ do you need, and how much?
Customer:	You sell it by the **3** _____ , don't you?
Clerk:	**4** _____ _____ .
Customer:	Good. I'll need twenty planks that are ten yards each. Also, how many red clay bricks are on **5** _____ _____ ?
Clerk:	There are **6** _____ _____ standard size bricks on a pallet.

Speaking

8 With a partner, act out the roles below based on Task 7. Then, switch roles.

Student A: You are a customer. Talk to Student B about:
- ordering building materials
- how the company sells the materials
- how much of the materials you need

Student B: You are a clerk for a building materials company. Talk to Student A about ordering materials.

Writing

9 Use the flyer and the conversation from Task 8 to fill out the order invoice.

lumber

PF Building Materials

Order Invoice

Customer: _____

Item ordered: Quantity:

_____   _____

_____   _____

Order ready: _____

_____

Properties and Dimensions

HOME PRODUCT GUIDE SERVICES CONTACT

BD
WINDOW COMPANY

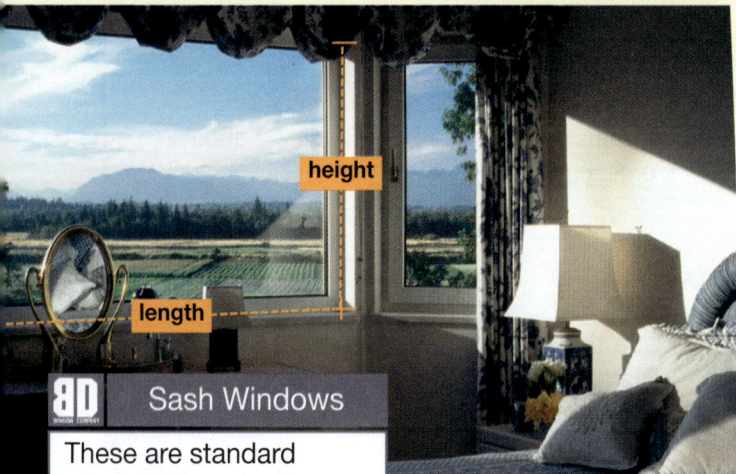

height

length

Sash Windows

These are standard windows for a home. Their typical **dimensions** are a **width** of 60cm and a **height** of 90 cm. The bottom sash opens. The top sash is fixed.

Storm Windows

These are a greater **weight** and provide extra **strength** to resist wind and other weather. They have a 3 cm **thickness**. We start at a minimum window **length** of 80 cm.

Casement Windows

These windows also have a sash. It swings inward or outward. They should be installed on a **sill** with a minimum length of 8 cm.

French Doors

We cut custom glass to fit French doors. They do require a minimum **jamb** width of 8 cm. The **depth** at the bottom of the door should be 1 cm.

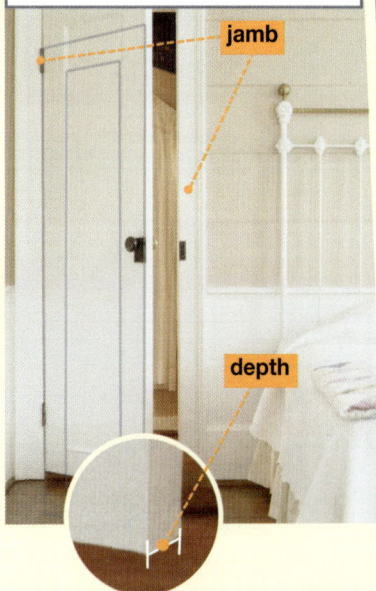

jamb

depth

Get ready!

1 Before you read the passage, talk about these questions.

1 What are some important dimensions in construction work?

2 What forms the base of a window?

Reading

2 Read the website from a window manufacturer. Then, mark the statements as true (T) or false (F).

1 __ The top sash opens in a standard sash window.

2 __ Casement window sills require an eight centimeter jamb.

3 __ French doors should have a jamb at least 8 cm wide.

Vocabulary

3 Match the words (1-5) with the definitions (A-E).

1 __ weight   3 __ length   5 __ width
2 __ depth   4 __ height

A the measurement of how long something is
B the measurement of how heavy something is
C the measurement of how wide something is
D the measurement of how deep something is
E the measurement of how tall something is

4 Fill in the blanks with the correct words from the word bank.

word BANK

thickness   sill   strength
dimensions   jamb

1 Steel has much more _____ than wood.

2 Don't place that bowl on the window _____ or it will fall off.

3 What is the height and other _____ of that table?

4 The window glass should have a _____ of at least 3cm to keep out cold winds.

5 This door will not fit inside its _____ .

5 🎧 Listen and read the website from a window manufacturer again. What dimensions are provided for the windows?

Listening

6 🎧 Listen to a conversation between two construction workers. Choose the correct answers.

1 What is the conversation mainly about?
   A adding an additional window
   B increasing the size of a window
   C measuring the size of a window
   D cutting out a new window sill

2 What will the workers likely do next?
   A install the window
   B call the homeowner
   C measure the dimensions of the wall
   D measure the dimensions of the window

7 🎧 Listen again and complete the conversation.

Worker 1: Rachel, I just **1** _____ _____ _____ from the homeowner.

Worker 2: Oh, really? What **2** _____ _____ _____ ?

Worker 1: He wants a **3** _____ _____ in the living room.

Worker 2: Okay. What's the **4** _____ _____ _____ ?

Worker 1: Well, **5** _____ _____ _____ one meter and the width was two meters. Now it's going to be one and a half meters tall and two and a quarter meters wide.

Worker 2: Wow, that's a large window!

Worker 1: Yeah, we'll have to **6** _____ _____ _____ to see if it'll fit.

sill

Speaking

8 With a partner, act out the roles below based on Task 7. Then, switch roles.

USE LANGUAGE SUCH AS:

S/he wants a ...
The height was ...
Now it's going to ...

Student A: You are a construction worker. Talk to Student B about:
• a change in a window size
• what the old size was
• what the new size should be

Student B: You are a construction worker. Talk to Student A about a window.

Writing

9 Use the website and the conversation from Task 8 to fill out the work order change.

8D Window Company
Work Order Change

Client: _____

Change requested: _____
_____

Old Dimensions
   Height: _____
   Width: _____

New Dimensions
   Height: _____
   Width: _____

27

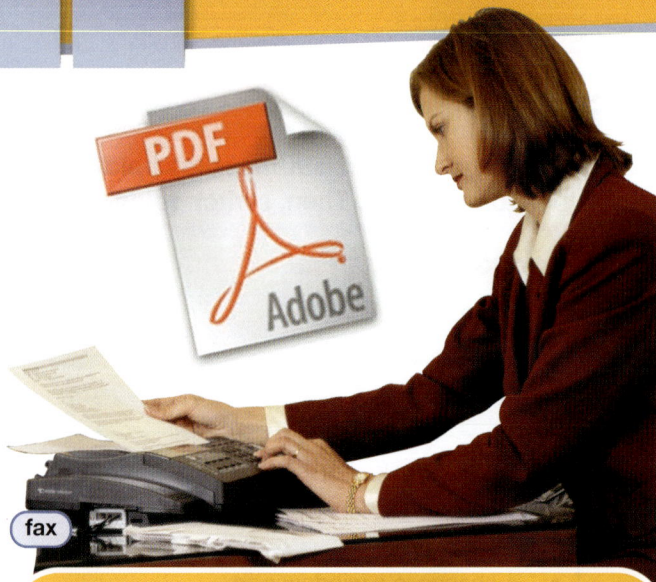

fax

Stetson ELECTRONICS

Business Communication Solutions

At Stetson Electronics we offer a variety of devices for a construction company. Our selection of modern **two-way radios** are easy to use. Their range covers any job site, large or small.

Our **smartphones** improve **communications**. **Contact** workers at a job site. Send and receive **emails** and **PDF** documents. **Scan** blueprints at the office and send them to a phone on-site. **Confirm** directions with the touch of a button. With a smartphone, you may never need to **fax** a document again!

So come to Stetson Electronics. **Consult** our staff about what would work best for you!

two-way radio

email

Get ready!

1 Before you read the passage, talk about these questions.

1 What communication devices are used on a construction site?

2 How can a plan or drawing be sent to a smartphone?

Reading

2 Read the website for an electronics store. Then, mark the statements as true (T) or false (F).

1 __ A two-way radio's range may not cover large job sites.

2 __ Smartphones can scan blueprint images.

3 __ The company recommends faxing documents instead of emailing pdfs.

Vocabulary

3 Match the words (1-6) with the definitions (A-F).

1 __ contact   4 __ communication

2 __ fax   5 __ confirm

3 __ consult   6 __ scan

A to make an electronic copy of something

B to make sure a statement is true

C the sharing of information with someone

D to ask someone for their opinion or advice

E to begin exchanging messages with someone

F to use a machine that sends a document's information by telephone

4 Fill in the blanks with the correct words and phrases from the word bank.

WORD BANK

PDF   email   smartphone
two-way radio

1 Write a(n) _____ to the site manager.

2 Scan the blueprints as a(n) _____ .

3 A(n) _____ has a smaller range than a cell phone.

4 A(n) _____ has many more functions than a cell phone.

5 🎧 **Listen and read the website for an electronics store again. What are some of the features of smartphones?**

Listening

6 🎧 **Listen to a conversation between a construction company owner and a site manager. Choose the correct answers.**

1   What problem do the speakers discuss?

    A   They cannot find the blueprints.

    B   The size of the bathroom may change.

    C   They do not know the client's phone number.

    D   An employee cannot be reached at the job site.

2   What will the woman likely do next?

    A   call the client

    B   measure the bathroom

    C   leave for the job site

    D   change the blueprint

7 🎧 **Listen again and complete the conversation.**

Manager: Hopefully. I'm just **1** _____ _____ how big the bathroom should be.

Owner: You **2** _____ _____ the blueprint?

Manager: I do. But the architect might **3** _____ _____ _____ . He said he would contact you.

Owner: Okay. **4** _____ _____ _____ get you that information?

Manager: You could call me on my smartphone or **5** _____ _____ a PDF of the blueprint.

Owner: I'll send you the blueprint. Then you'll **6** _____ _____ _____ clearly.

scan

smartphone

Speaking

8 **With a partner, act out the roles below based on Task 7. Then, switch roles.**

USE LANGUAGE SUCH AS:

I'm just not sure ...

How should I ...?

You could ... or ...

Student A: You are a construction company owner. Talk to Student B about:

•   a possible change in a plan

•   options to tell Student B about the change

•   what option you will use

Student B: You are a construction site manager. Talk to Student A about a possible change in a plan.

Writing

9 **Use the website and the conversation from Task 8 to fill out the company owner's daily planner.**

Daily Planner

Date: _____

Tasks to do:

* Contact _____ about _____ .

* Call _____ _____ . Tell her _____
_____ .

bathroom · living room · garage · walk-in closet · patio

Shady Pines
A Luxury Housing Community

Ready to put a **roof** over your head?

Shady Pines has homes for families of all sizes. Look at our most popular models.

Model / Starting Price: Oak—$150,000

- 2 **bedrooms**/1 **bathroom**
- Spacious **living room**
- Cozy **kitchen**
- 1-car **garage**
- **Utility room** with extra storage space

Model / Starting Price: Maple—$200,000

- **Master bedroom** with **walk-in closet**, plus two additional bedrooms
- 3 bathrooms
- Huge kitchen and living room
- Utility room with appliances
- 2-car garage

Model / Starting Price: Evergreen—$275,000

- Master bedroom, plus four more bedrooms—all with walk-in closets!
- 4 bathrooms
- Huge living room and kitchen with appliances, both with great views
- Utility room with appliances
- 2-car garage
- Landscaped backyard with **patio** and/or pool (optional)

Get ready!

❶ Before you read the passage, talk about these questions.

1 In which area of a house is a car parked?

2 What feature is located at the back of a house?

Reading

❷ Read the advertisement from a new housing community. Then, choose the correct answers.

1 What is the advertisement mostly about?

   A the size of different rooms

   B a tour of a redesigned home

   C the features of different houses

   D room improvements the company provides

2 What is NOT a difference between the Oak and Maple models?

   A Oak has fewer bedrooms.

   B Maple has two more bathrooms.

   C Oak has utility room appliances.

   D Maple has additional garage space.

3 What is true of Evergreen models?

   A Their patios are bigger than Maple's.

   B They do not all have pools.

   C Their bedrooms all have bathrooms.

   D Their living rooms have appliances.

Vocabulary

❸ Check (✓) the sentence that uses the underlined part correctly.

1 __ **A** The room has a <u>walk-in closet</u> where you can hang all your clothes.

   __ **B** We park our cars in the <u>utility room</u> at night.

2 __ **A** He watches TV in the <u>bathroom</u> after dinner.

   __ **B** They eat dinner outside on the <u>patio</u> when the weather is warm.

3 __ **A** The house has several leaks in the <u>roof</u>.

   __ **B** They got a new oven for the <u>living room</u>.

4 __ **A** The <u>bedrooms</u> are on the second floor of the house.

   __ **B** The <u>garage</u> has a walk-in closet and bathroom attached.

4 Fill in the blanks with the correct words and phrases from the word bank.

bathroom   master bedroom   kitchen
garage   utility room   living room

1 The client asked for the _____ to be designed large enough for her bed and dresser.

2 The washer and dryer are in the _____ .

3 The _____ needs a gas line for the stove and oven.

4 The _____ has two sinks and a large walk-in shower.

5 There are two couches and an armchair in the _____ .

6 The _____ has enough room for two cars.

5 🎧 Listen and read the advertisement for a new housing community again. Which house would be best for a young couple?

Listening

6 🎧 Listen to a conversation between a construction company owner and a manager. Mark the following statements as true (T) or false (F).

1 __ The woman wants to add walk-in closets.

2 __ The man suggests making the utility room smaller.

3 __ The man wants to expand the kitchen into the living room.

7 🎧 Listen again and complete the conversation.

Owner:	Let's **1** _____ _____ the plans for the model home.
Manager:	Sure. Construction starts in **2** _____ _____ .
Owner:	Right. Now, the master bedroom has a walk-in closet. But I think the **3** _____ walk-in closets, too.
Manager:	I **4** _____ _____ . Homeowners love closet space.
Owner:	Yes, they do. We can just make the **5** _____ a little smaller.
Manager:	**6** _____ _____ . People also like big kitchens.

Speaking

8 With a partner, act out the roles below based on Task 7. Then, switch roles.

USE LANGUAGE SUCH AS:

But I think…
I agree completely.
That's a great idea.

Student A: You are the owner of a construction company. Talk to Student B about:

- the features of your model home
- what home buyers want to see
- changes to make to a model home

Student B: You are a site manager. Talk to Student A about changes to the model home.

Writing

9 Use the advertisement and the conversation from Task 8 to fill out the advertisement.

Come See Our Model Home!

Rooms: _____
_____
_____
_____

Features: _____
_____
_____

Come See Our ModelHome!

15 Parts of a Commercial Building

← **EMERGENCY EXIT**

stairwell

FIRE ESCAPE →

EXIT →

office

ELEVATOR

lobby

Get ready!

1 Before you read the passage, talk about these questions.

1 How can people move between floors in a building?

2 What are two safety features of a building?

Reading

2 Read the email to a construction company manager. Then, choose the correct answers.

1 What is the purpose of the email?
   - **A** to say what different types of signs are needed
   - **B** to describe how the office will look
   - **C** to give instructions on where to put signs
   - **D** to explain what to do in an emergency

2 What can you infer about the location of the back exit?
   - **A** It is near the stairwell.
   - **B** It is far from the lobby.
   - **C** It is located on the second floor.
   - **D** It can be reached from the east hallway.

3 Which of the following is NOT labeled an exit for emergencies?
   - **A** lobby entrance
   - **C** fire escape
   - **B** back exit
   - **D** elevator

From:	susan.hererra@p&jlaw.com
To:	r_taylor@constructionco.com
Subject:	New building

Dear Richard,

The new **office** is almost finished. So let's talk about the finishing touches. Specifically, I want to address the **exit signs**.

On the first **floor**, put a sign pointing to the **entrance** in the **lobby**. We need another one in the east **hallway**. That way, people know about the back **exit** in an **emergency**. On the second floor, put signs over the windows leading to the **fire escape**. In addition, put signs near the entrance to the **stairwell**. We'll need another sign near the **elevator**. It should point to the stairwell. We don't want people to use the elevator in an emergency, and that's the closest exit.

If you have questions, please call me.

Thanks,
Susan Hererra

hallway

fire escape

Vocabulary

3 Fill in the blanks with the correct words and phrases from the word bank.

WORD BANK

office   floor   entrance
stairwell   exit sign

1 The company's old _____ was small and dark, but the new one is much nicer.

2 The _____ pointed to the doors at the end of the hallway.

3 The accounting department is on the second _____ .

4 The elevator broke, so everyone had to go up the _____ .

5 After-hours visitors can only get into the building using the south _____ .

4 Read the sentence pairs. Choose which word or phrase best fits each blank.

1 elevator / lobby

  A Offices with multiple floors usually have a(n) _____ as well as stairs.

  B The _____ is the first room people enter.

2 hallway / fire escape

  A The employees climbed out the window onto the
  _____ .

  B The meeting room is at the end of the _____ on the left side.

3 exit / emergency

  A There's an _____ on the second floor. Call the fire department.

  B The _____ was blocked, people couldn't exit the building.

5 🎧 Listen and read the email to a construction company manager again. What kind of sign is needed near an elevator?

Listening

6 🎧 Listen to a conversation between an office manager and a construction worker. Mark the following statements as true (T) or false (F).

1 ___ The woman is hanging signs at multiple exits.

2 ___ The building does not have a fire escape.

3 ___ The man wants a sign directing people to the elevator.

7 🎧 Listen again and complete the conversation.

Manager:	Hi, Rachel. You're hanging exit signs in the **1** _____ _____ today, right?
Worker:	Yes. I'm labeling the north and east **2** _____ right now.
Manager:	Great! Did you put one near the **3** _____ _____ ?
Worker:	Yes, **4** _____ _____ .
Manager:	Okay. And have you put a sign near the elevator **5** _____ ?
Worker:	No, **6** _____ _____ . You wanted one there?
Manager:	Yes. Something that says not to use the elevator during a fire.
Worker:	You got it. I'll hang a sign that points to the stairwell.

Speaking

8 With a partner, act out the roles below based on Task 7. Then, switch roles.

USE LANGUAGE SUCH AS:

Did you ...?

Have you ... yet?

Yes, I did.

No, I haven't.

Student A: You are an office manager. Talk to Student B about:

• what types of signs are needed

• where he or she should put the signs

Student B: You are a construction worker. Talk to Student A about the signs for his or her office building.

Writing

9 Use the email and the conversation from Task 8 to fill out an inspector's survey of an office building.

Inspection of Office Signage

Date of inspection: _____

Company name: _____

Office manager: _____

Where are the exit signs located in the building?

_____

_____

_____

Glossary

add [V-T-U8] To **add** numbers is to combine them.

adjustable wrench [N-COUNT-U2] An **adjustable wrench** is a wrench with an opening that can be changed in size.

air compressor [N-COUNT-U3] An **air compressor** is a tool that creates energy by increasing pressure on gas or electrical power and releases it in short bursts. This energy is used to power other devices.

anchor [N-COUNT-U4] An **anchor** is a fastener often used when screws, nails, or other fasteners are impractical or ineffective.

bathroom [N-COUNT-U14] A **bathroom** is a room where people use the toilet and take a shower or bath.

bedroom [N-COUNT-U14] A **bedroom** is a room where a person sleeps.

bolt [N-COUNT-U4] A **bolt** is a metal fastener with a threaded body that is held in place with a nut on the end opposite the head.

box-end wrench [N-COUNT-U2] A **box-end wrench** is a wrench with an enclosed opening that grasps the face of a bolt.

brad [N-COUNT-U4] A **brad** is a thin, small nail with a slight projection at the top on one side.

brick [N-COUNT-U11] **Brick** is a building material made of rectangular blocks of hardened clay.

cement mixer [N-COUNT-U3] A **cement mixer** is a machine that combines the components that make cement in a large circular barrel that rotates.

center [V-T-U7] To **center** something is to move it so that it is in the middle of an area.

centimeter [N-COUNT-U10] A **centimeter** is a metric unit of length equal to 1/100th of a meter.

chalk line reel [N-COUNT-U2] A **chalk line reel** is a tool for marking a long, straight line on a flat surface.

check [V-T-U7] To **check** something is to make sure it is correct.

cinder block [N-COUNT-U11] A **cinder block** is a lightweight building block made from concrete.

circular saw [N-COUNT-U3] A **circular saw** is a tool that uses a rotating metal disk with sharp teeth to cut through wood or metal.

claw hammer [N-COUNT-U1] A **claw hammer** is a tool used to insert nails into a wall or other object.

come to [PHR V-T-U8] To **come to** an amount is to add up to that amount.

communication [N-UNCOUNT-U13] **Communication** is sharing information with someone.

compactor [N-COUNT-U3] A **compactor** is a machine that bounces on the ground to compact soil.

concrete [N-UNCOUNT-U11] **Concrete** is a mix of cement, water, gravel, and sand used as a building material.

confirm [V-T-U13] To **confirm** a statement is to make sure it is true.

consult [V-T-U13] To **consult** someone is to ask him or her for his or her opinion or advice.

contact [V-T-U13] To **contact** someone is to begin exchanging messages with him or her.

convert [V-T-U9] To **convert** a number is to change it from a fraction into a decimal, or vice versa.

cut [V-T-U6] To **cut** something is to divide it with a sharp instrument such as a saw.

decimal [N-COUNT-U9] A **decimal** is a number with digits to the right of a decimal point, expressing part of a whole number.

denominator [N-COUNT-U9] A **denominator** is the bottom number of a fraction.

depth [N-UNCOUNT-U12] **Depth** is the distance measurement of something from its front to its back or its bottom to its top.

dimensions [N-PLURAL-U12] **Dimensions** are basic physical properties of an object, such as height, width, or weight.

divide by [V-T-U8] To **divide** one number **by** another is to split the first number into an equal number of parts.

drill [V-T-U6] To **drill** something is to create a hole in it by using a drill.

drywall [N-UNCOUNT-U11] **Drywall** is a building material that consists of gypsum between heavy sheets of paper, used for interior walls.

dust mask [N-COUNT-U5] A **dust mask** is a partial face-covering that prevents the wearer from getting dust particles in his or her nose or mouth.

earplugs [N-PLURAL-U5] **Earplugs** (also ear plugs) are small, flexible pieces of rubber or plastic that are put in the ears to protect them from loud noises.

elevator [N-COUNT-U15] An **elevator** is a machine that moves up and down, carrying people and things between floors of a building.

email [N-COUNT-U13] An **email** is a digital text message, similar to a letter, but sent through the Internet.

emergency [N-COUNT-U15] An **emergency** is an unexpected situation that requires instant action.

entrance [N-COUNT-U15] An **entrance** is a door that people use to go into a building or room.

equal [V-I-U8] To **equal** a number is to have the same value as it.

exit [N-COUNT-U15] An **exit** is a door that people use to leave a building or room.

exit sign [N-COUNT-U15] An **exit sign** is a sign that indicates where a person can go to get out of a building.

face shield [N-COUNT-U5] A **face shield** is a piece of safety equipment, typically made of plastic, glass, or wire, that protects the entire face from dangers like flying objects.

fax [V-T-U13] To **fax** a document is to send a copy of it using a machine that sends information by telephone.

fire escape [N-COUNT-U15] A **fire escape** is an emergency exit from a building. Usually it consists of a staircase on the outside of a building that a person can get onto via a window.

first aid kit [N-COUNT-U5] A **first aid kit** is a container that has all of the basic supplies needed to treat a minor injury.

flathead screwdriver [N-COUNT-U1] A **flathead screwdriver** is a tool used to turn slotted screws.

floor [N-COUNT-U15] A **floor** is a level of a building where there are usually many different rooms.

flooring [N-UNCOUNT-U11] **Flooring** is the material used in floors.

foot [N-COUNT-U10] A **foot** is an imperial unit of length, equal to 12 inches.

fraction [N-COUNT-U9] A **fraction** is a ratio of two numbers, expressed with one number written above the other.

gallon [N-COUNT-U10] A **gallon** is the basic imperial unit of volume.

garage [N-COUNT-U14] A **garage** is the part of a house where people park cars.

glass [N-UNCOUNT-U11] **Glass** is a solid, breakable, and transparent material often used to make windows.

goggles [N-PLURAL-U5] **Goggles** are a type of protective eyewear that cover the eyes and the area around them. They protect the eyes from particles that may fly out while using power tools or doing construction work.

grade [N-UNCOUNT-U4] **Grade** is a measurement of a bolt's strength, usually stamped on the bolt's head.

grip gloves [N-PLURAL-U5] **Grip gloves** are gloves that have a rubbery coating on the outside, which allows the user to hold onto things more firmly.

hacksaw [N-COUNT-U1] A **hacksaw** is a tool with a blade generally used for cutting metal.

hallway [N-COUNT-U15] A **hallway** is typically a long passageway that connects rooms.

hammer drill [N-COUNT-U3] A **hammer drill** is a tool that makes holes in hard surfaces like stone by using a rotating drill bit and applying force in a back-and-forth motion.

hand saw [N-COUNT-U1] A **hand saw** is a saw with a handle and a broad semi-flexible metal blade with small teeth for cutting wood.

hard hat [N-COUNT-U5] A **hard hat** is a helmet made of metal or plastic that protects the head on construction sites.

height [N-UNCOUNT-U12] **Height** is the measurement from the bottom to the top of something.

Glossary

imperial [ADJ-U10] If a measurement is imperial, it is from the English System of measurement, mostly used in the United States today.

inch [N-COUNT-U10] An inch is the basic imperial unit of length.

insert [V-T-U7] To insert something is to put it inside something else.

jackhammer [N-COUNT-U3] A jackhammer is a tool that breaks up very hard surfaces like rock or pavement.

jamb [N-UNCOUNT-U12] A jamb is a vertical part of a door or window frame.

kilogram [N-COUNT-U10] A kilogram is the basic metric unit of mass, equal to one thousand grams.

kitchen [N-COUNT-U14] A kitchen is a room where people cook and sometimes eat.

kneepads [N-PLURAL-U5] Kneepads are a type of protective equipment that provide cushioning to protect the knees in the case of a fall and provide comfort when doing tasks that involve kneeling.

leather gloves [N-PLURAL-U5] Leather gloves are a type of safety equipment that protect the hands while doing hazardous work.

length [N-UNCOUNT-U12] Length is the measurement of something along its longest side.

level [N-COUNT-U1] A level is a tool used to measure how flat something is.

lift [V-T-U6] To lift something is to pick it up.

line up [PHRASAL V-U7] To line up an object with something else is to place it so that certain parts of each object are in the correct place.

liter [N-COUNT-U10] A liter is the basic metric unit of volume.

living room [N-COUNT-U14] A living room is a room intended for socializing or entertaining.

lobby [N-COUNT-U15] A lobby is a room located at the entrance of a building.

loosen [V-T-U7] To loosen something is to turn it to make it easier to remove.

lumber [N-UNCOUNT-U11] Lumber is processed wood used as a building material.

mark [V-T-U6] To mark something is to write a sign on it for reference.

master bedroom [N-COUNT-U14] A master bedroom is usually the biggest bedroom in a house. Typically, this is where the owner of the house sleeps.

measure [V-T-U6] To measure something is to calculate the size or quantity of it.

meter [N-COUNT-U10] A meter is the basic metric unit of length.

metric [ADJ-U10] If a measurement is metric, it is from the International System of Measurement, used in many countries today.

metric thread [N-UNCOUNT-U4] Metric thread is measurement of a screw's thread in the metric system.

minus [PREP-U8] Minus is used to show that one number is being removed from another.

mixed number [N-COUNT-U9] A mixed number is a number that contains a whole number and a fraction.

multiply [V-T-U8] To multiply a number is to add it to itself a number of times.

nail [N-COUNT-U4] A nail is a metal fastener shaped like a spike, driven into place with a hammer.

nail [V-T-U6] To nail something is to attach it to something else using a nail.

nail gun [N-COUNT-U3] A nail gun is a device that puts nails into a hard material, like wood, when the user pulls a trigger.

needle-nose pliers [N-PLURAL-U1] Needle-nose pliers are hand tools with long, narrow extensions on the end, used to reach into narrow gaps.

numerator [N-COUNT-U9] A numerator is the upper number of a fraction.

nut [N-COUNT-U4] A nut is a piece of metal with a hole through it and internal threads, that screws onto a bolt.

office [N-COUNT-U15] An office is a room in which a person does his or her work.

open-end wrench [N-COUNT-U2] An open-end wrench is a wrench that has a U-shaped opening at the end to grasp opposite sides of a bolt.

patio [N-COUNT-U14] A patio is an outdoor area next to a house where people sometimes eat or relax.

PDF [ABBREV-U13] A PDF (Portable Document Format) is a computer document that can be displayed on any kind of computer, independent of hardware or software.

percent [N-COUNT-U9] A percent is a number that expresses a part of something per hundred.

percentage [N-COUNT-U9] A percentage is the amount of something expressed as part of one hundred.

Phillips screwdriver [N-COUNT-U1] A Phillips screwdriver is a tool used to turn Phillips screws, which have two short slots that meet at a right angle.

place [V-T-U6] To place something is to set it somewhere.

plastic [N-UNCOUNT-U11] Plastic is a manmade material made of organic compounds that can be easily molded into many shapes.

plumb bob [N-COUNT-U2] A plumb bob is a weight attached to a line used to determine if something is perpendicular to something else.

plus [PREP-U8] Plus is used to show that two numbers are being combined.

pound [N-COUNT-U10] A pound is the basic imperial unit of mass.

power drill [N-COUNT-U3] A power drill is an electrically powered tool that makes holes in surfaces by rotating a drill bit.

push [V-T-U6] To push something is to apply force to it so that it moves away.

rebar [N-COUNT-U11] A rebar is a steel bar used to reinforce concrete and masonry structures.

reciprocating saw [N-COUNT-U3] A reciprocating saw is an electrically powered tool that cuts through surfaces using a blade that moves back and forth.

reduce [V-T-U9] To reduce a fraction is to divide the numerator and denominator by the same number until they can no longer be divided into whole numbers.

remainder [N-COUNT-U8] A remainder is the number that is left over after a division operation which does not divide into equal parts.

remove [V-T-U7] To remove something is to take it out of something else.

repeat [V-T-U6] To repeat an action is to do it again.

roof [N-COUNT-U14] A roof is a structure that covers a house or building.

round up [V-T-U8] To round up a number is to increase it to a greater whole number.

rubber [N-UNCOUNT-U11] Rubber is a bendable material that is either manmade or comes from the sap of the rubber tree.

safety glasses [N-PLURAL-U5] Safety glasses are a type of protective eyewear which have plastic lenses that will not shatter.

sander [N-COUNT-U3] A sander is an electrically powered tool that uses sandpaper to make wooden and metal surfaces smooth.

scan [V-T-U13] To scan something is to make an electronic copy of it.

screw [N-COUNT-U4] A screw is a metal fastener with a threaded shank, driven into place with a screwdriver.

screw [V-T-U6] To screw something is to connect it to something else using a screw.

sill [N-COUNT-U12] A sill is a horizontal bar that forms the base of a window.

sledgehammer [N-COUNT-U2] A sledgehammer is a hammer with a large, flat head made of metal, giving it a very powerful force when used.

Glossary

slide [V-T-U7] To **slide** something is to push it horizontally along the surface of something else.

slip-joint pliers [N-PLURAL-U1] **Slip-joint pliers** are hand tools with parallel, flat pincers used for gripping small objects. Slip-joint pliers also have an adjustable slot that allows the pliers to increase the opening of the jaws.

smartphone [N-COUNT-U13] A **smartphone** is a mobile phone that has advanced features such as Internet access and touchscreen controls.

snips [N-PLURAL-U2] **Snips** are strong scissors used to cut sheet metal or similar materials.

socket [N-COUNT-U2] A **socket** is a head that attaches to a wrench for tightening different sized bolts.

socket wrench [N-COUNT-U2] A **socket wrench** is a wrench with heads that are attached to a fitting and can be changed.

speed square [N-COUNT-U2] A **speed square** is a triangle-shaped tool used to draw straight lines and angles.

stairwell [N-COUNT-U15] A **stairwell** is the space where the stairs are in a building.

staple [N-COUNT-U4] A **staple** is a U-shaped metal or wire fastener used to hold something together by penetrating it and curling around it.

steel [N-UNCOUNT-U11] **Steel** is a strong metal alloy made of iron and carbon.

steel-toe boots [N-PLURAL-U5] **Steel-toe boots** are boots that have extra reinforcement at the toe, typically a plate made of steel. This protects the wearer's feet from heavy falling objects.

strength [N-UNCOUNT-U12] **Strength** is the measurement of how powerful something is or how much resistance it has.

subtract [V-T-U8] To **subtract** a number is to reduce a second number by that amount.

support [V-T-U7] To **support** something is to keep it from falling down.

tape measure [N-COUNT-U1] A **tape measure** is a tool used to determine the length of something.

thickness [N-UNCOUNT-U12] **Thickness** is the distance measurement of something from one surface to the other.

tighten [V-T-U7] To **tighten** something is to make it tighter and harder to remove.

tool box [N-COUNT-U1] A **tool box** is a portable container used to carry tools.

total [V-T-U8] If something **totals** something else, it comes to that amount.

turn [V-T-U7] To **turn** something is to change its direction.

twist [V-T-U7] To **twist** something is to cause it to rotate.

two-way radio [N-COUNT-U13] A **two-way radio** is a radio that can both send and receive information over broadcast signals.

utility knife [N-COUNT-U1] A **utility knife** is a small tool used to cut various materials, such as cardboard or rope.

utility room [N-COUNT-U14] A **utility room** is a room where people do laundry and store items that do not get used every day.

UTS thread [N-UNCOUNT-U4] **UTS thread** (**Unified Thread Standard thread**) is a measurement of a screw's thread.

walk-in closet [N-COUNT-U14] A **walk-in closet** is a place where people store clothes. These rooms are usually big enough for a person to walk around in them.

washer [N-COUNT-U4] A **washer** is a flat disk placed beneath a nut to distribute pressure and prevent leaking.

weight [N-UNCOUNT-U12] **Weight** is the measurement of how heavy something is.

whole number [N-COUNT-U9] A **whole number** is a number that is not divided into parts.

width [N-UNCOUNT-U12] **Width** is the distance measurement of something from one side of it to the other.

yard [N-COUNT-U10] A **yard** is an imperial measurement of length equal to three feet.

Career Paths

Construction I

Buildings

Book
2

Virginia Evans

Jenny Dooley

Jason Revels

Express Publishing

Scope and Sequence

Unit	Topic	Reading context	Vocabulary	Function
1	Careers	Job listings	carpenter, contractor, electrician, foreman, HVAC technician, laborer, mason, painter, roofer, semiskilled, skilled, subcontractor, unskilled	Describing experience
2	Worksite Safety	Worksite safety poster	4:1 rule, accident, class, closed space, fall, ground, ladder, Material Safety Data Sheet, pump jack, scaffold, toxic, trench safety, ventilation	Expressing dissatisfaction
3	Site Investigation	Letter	clay, drill rig, gravel, level, sand, silt, soil profile, subsurface investigation, surface evaluation, test pit, topographic survey	Asking about requirements
4	Site Layout	Email	batter board, bench mark, builder's level, grade rod, horizontal, monument, property line, run, site plan, stake, utilities, wire	Explaining the order of events
5	Cranes	Brochure	crawler crane, disassembly, mobile crane, operator's cab, outrigger, secure, stabilizer, stationary crane, tower crane, truck mounted crane	Asking for advice
6	Rigging	Instructions	birdcage, chain sling, charred, core, fatigue, kink, knot, lay, link, rigging, sling, strand nicking, web sling, wire rope	Describing damage
7	Excavation 1	Email	dewatering system, drill, excavation, extract, groundwater, pump, runoff, sump, water table, well-point	Selecting an option
8	Excavation 2	Website	concrete slurry, deposit, dig, general excavation, haul, interlocking sheet piling, payline, sloping, soil swell, special excavation, steel soldier piles, tieback, timber lagging	Discussing an option
9	Foundations 1	Website	building load, footing, foundation, freeze, grade beam, monolithic foundation, pier, residential, shallow foundation, spread foundation, stem wall, thaw	Discussing pros and cons
10	Foundations 2	Textbook	bearing pile, caisson, cast-in-place pile, deep foundation, drilled foundation, driven foundation, friction pile, friction plus bearing pile, pile, pile driver, sheet pile	Expressing confusion
11	Formwork 1	Advertisement	consolidation, cure, design strength, formwork, framing, lightweight, mold, prefabricated, reuse, strip, temporary	Describing progress
12	Formwork 2	Article	brace, footing form, line, modular system, permanent insulated formwork, plywood, sheathing, stay-in-place, stud, tie-spreader unit, wale, wall form	Asking about chronological order
13	Floor Plans	Website	appliance, bird's-eye-view, building layout, diagram, dimensions, fixture, floor plan, function, indicate, interior, placement, specify	Asking for more detail
14	Floors 1	Email	beam, diaphragm, floor, joist, joist connection, mudsill, parallel, platform framing, span, subfloor, support, truss	Describing a problem
15	Floors 2	Textbook	above grade, anchor, beam-and-slab, concrete floor, construction joint, cross-braced, drop panel, high-rise, lateral stability, one-way joist slab, one-way solid slab, post-tensioned, span, structural slab, tendon, two-way flat plate slab, two-way solid slab	Reacting to good news

Table of Contents

carpenter

electrician

mason

painter

roofer

JOS **Contractors** is taking applications for three **skilled** positions: **carpenter**, **electrician**, and **HVAC technician**. Applicants must be fully licensed with three years of work experience. We will also consider forming **subcontractor** partnerships with established businesses. Submit a resume and cover letter to aschmitt@joscontractors.biz.

AUK Construction seeks **semiskilled roofers**, **painters**, and **masons**. We will provide training. This is a valuable opportunity to gain on-the-job work experience. However, applicants should have some experience in construction. Send references and work history to btaylor@aukconstruction.com.

TPX Management is hiring **unskilled laborers** for general work at a construction site. Workers must be able to lift more than 25 kilograms. If interested, please call (643) 555-5648. We are also seeking a **foreman** to lead this crew. The ideal candidate should have at least two years' previous supervisory experience. Submit a resume and cover letter to pcalhoun@tpxmgmt.org.

Get ready!

1 Before you read the passage, talk about these questions.

1 What are some different construction careers?
2 What material does a carpenter work with?

Reading

2 Read the job listings for construction companies. Then, choose the correct answers.

1 What is a requirement for being hired by JOS Contractors?

A being fully licensed
B being able to lift 25 kilograms
C having an established business
D having previous supervisory experience

2 Which of the following positions is AUK Construction NOT hiring?

A roofers   C painters
B masons   D carpenters

3 What position can a person with no experience apply for?

A painter   C foreman
B laborer   D subcontractor

Vocabulary

3 Match the words (1-7) with the definitions (A-G).

1 __ contractor   5 __ laborer
2 __ carpenter   6 __ electrician
3 __ foreman   7 __ mason
4 __ HVAC technician

A a person who uses physical strength and abilities to earn money

B a person skilled in installing and repairing heating, venting, and air conditioning systems

C a person who runs a company that is hired to build or repair a building

D a person who is trained to wire buildings and repair electrical problems

E a person who is trained to use wood to create buildings and other structures

F a person who builds structures with stone or brick

G the leader of a construction work crew

4 Fill in the blanks with the correct words: *roofer, semiskilled, painter, skilled, subcontractor, unskilled*.

1 The contractor hired a(n) _____ to install the HVAC system in the building.

2 An electrician is considered a(n) _____ professional.

3 Hire a(n) _____ to paint the exterior walls.

4 _____ workers usually have some training, but are paid less than highly-skilled workers.

5 The contractor used _____ workers to move building materials.

6 Call a(n) _____ to fix the damage to the roof.

5 🎧 **Listen and read the job listings for construction companies again. What kind of workers is TPX Management hiring?**

Listening

6 🎧 **Listen to a conversation between a construction company manager and a job applicant. Mark the following statements as true (T) or false (F).**

1 __ The woman worked at the same company for five years.

2 __ The woman was a foreman at an office building construction site.

3 __ The man has never been a foreman.

7 🎧 **Listen again and complete the conversation.**

Manager:	It's my pleasure. Could you tell me about your previous **1** _____ _____ ?
Applicant:	Sure. I've actually done a **2** _____ _____ _____ everything. Altogether I have about five years of experience as a foreman.
Manager:	I see. And that was for **3** _____ _____ ?
Applicant:	Yes. **4** _____ _____ , I was a foreman at the site of the new office building on Grand Avenue. AUK Construction built it.
Manager:	Ah, I know the one. How many workers did you **5** _____ there?
Applicant:	I was **6** _____ _____ _____ most of the unskilled laborers. There were about twenty on **7** _____ _____ _____ .
Manager:	That sounds like a lot to handle. What was your greatest challenge?
Applicant:	Just making sure everyone was in the right place at the right time. You know, doing their jobs but also being safe.

Speaking

8 With a partner, act out the roles below based on Task 7. Then, switch roles.

USE LANGUAGE SUCH AS:

I have ...

For example ...

What was your greatest challenge ...?

Student A: You are a construction company manager. Talk to Student B about:

- experience needed for a job
- a specific job Student B has done
- the biggest challenge at a previous job

Student B: You are a job applicant. Talk to Student A about experience needed for a job.

Writing

9 Use the job listings and the conversation from Task 8 to fill out the job applicant evaluation.

TPX Management

Job Applicant Evaluation

Applicant: _____

Position: _____

Experience: _____

_____

Previous job: _____

_____

Biggest challenge: _____

_____

scaffold

trench safety

ladder

Worksite Safety

NOTICE

Follow the guidelines below at all times. In the event of an **accident**, notify a supervisor and call emergency services.

- When working on **ladders**, follow the **4:1 rule**. Avoid **falls** from **scaffolds** and **pump jacks** by wearing a safety harness. Pay attention to the platform's weight limit. Exceeding that limit can cause a collapse.

- Ensure proper **ventilation** when working with **toxic** chemicals in **closed spaces**. Read the **Material Safety Data Sheets** (MSDS) thoroughly and take all recommended precautions.

- Know the causes of each **class** of fire and the correct type of extinguisher to use on each type. Keep fire extinguishers on hand for Class A and B fires.

- Never take water near an electrical **ground**. Wear rubber-soled boots to protect against electric shock.

- Practice good **trench safety**. Never stack equipment or pile dirt near trench edges.

Get ready!

1 **Before you read the passage, talk about these questions.**

1 What equipment allows workers to climb higher on a building?

2 What is an accident that can happen to a worker when using a ladder?

Reading

2 **Read the poster on worksite safety. Then, mark the statements as true (T) or false (F).**

1 __ Not following the 4:1 rule can cause a scaffold to collapse.

2 __ Different classes of fire need different types of fire extinguishers.

3 __ Not wearing rubber-soled boots violates trench safety.

Vocabulary

3 **Fill in the blanks with the correct words and phrases from the word bank.**

WORD BANK

toxic	trench safety	4:1 rule
pump jack	Material Safety Data Sheet	

1 According to the _____ , you should wash your eyes thoroughly if the chemical gets in your eyes.

2 Position the ladder according to the _____ .

3 Most deaths occur when the walls cave in, so it is important to follow _____ guidelines.

4 When he finished installing the windows, Tim lowered the _____ to the ground.

5 This substance is _____ and will cause illnesses if inhaled.

4 **Read the sentence pairs. Choose which word or phrase best fits each blank.**

1 **class / accident**

A The _____ A fire occurred when a piece of paper got too close to a stove.

B An employee broke his leg in the _____ at the construction site.

2 **scaffold / fall**

A Avoid a _____ by wearing a safety harness.

B John stood on a _____ that was fifteen feet off the ground.

3 **ground / ladder**

A The _____ was a metal rod installed into the foundation of the building.

B Use a _____ to repair the gutter on the roof.

4 **closed space / ventilation**

A Keep the window open to ensure proper _____ .

B Never use a toxic chemical in a _____ .

5 🎧 Listen and read the poster on worksite safety again. Where is proper ventilation very important?

Listening

6 🎧 Listen to a conversation between a contractor and an employee. Mark the following statements as true (T) or false (F).

1 __ The woman was injured in a fall.
2 __ The woman was on the top step of her ladder.
3 __ The woman broke multiple safety rules.

7 🎧 Listen again and complete the conversation.

Employee: You wanted to see me, Mr. Jackson?

Contractor: Yes. I **1** _____ _____ what I just saw. You were standing on the **2** _____ _____ of your ladder.

Employee: Oh, sorry. It was **3** _____ _____ _____ _____ .

Contractor: It's basic ladder safety. You should never stand on the top step of a ladder. Never. It's **4** _____ _____ to fall.

Employee: I'm sorry. It won't happen again, Mr. Jackson.

Contractor: Okay. But we still **5** _____ _____ _____ . You didn't follow the **6** _____ _____ , either.

Employee: The 4:1 rule?

Contractor: Yes. For every four feet of height, you position your ladder one foot away from the wall.

Employee: Oh, okay. I was about eight feet up. So the ladder should be two feet away from the wall?

Contractor: Exactly. Make sure you follow it next time.

fall

Speaking

8 With a partner, act out the roles below based on Task 7. Then, switch roles.

USE LANGUAGE SUCH AS:

I can't believe what …
You should …
It won't happen again.

Student A: You are a contractor. Talk to Student B about:
• breaking safety rules
• possible results
• how to correct the situation

Student B: You work for a contractor. Talk to Student A about safety violations.

Writing

9 Use the poster and the conversation from Task 8 to complete the disciplinary write-up.

Disciplinary Write-Up

Employee name: _____

Date of incident: _____

Problem: _____
_____
_____

Steps taken to fix problem: ____
_____
_____

sand

drill rig

gravel

clay

silt

topographic survey

To: Reggie Muldoon   May 15
From: Jackie Sandburg, JOS Contractors

Mr. Muldoon,

Before we begin construction on your property, we must conduct a thorough site investigation. This letter explains the steps in that process.

First, we will do a complete **surface evaluation**. This will include a **topographic survey** of the surface features. The designers will use this data to design appropriate landscape features. We will also know if we need to move soil to make the site **level**.

Next, a **subsurface investigation** will be necessary. We need to know what kind of soil the foundation will rest on. A preliminary check showed mostly **sand** and larger pieces of **gravel**. However, there may also be weaker **silt** or **clay** soils present. We will dig several **test pits** to obtain a complete **soil profile**. Some of these will only be a few meters deep. For others we will use a **drill rig** to dig twenty meters down.

Please let me know if you have any questions.

Regards,
Jackie Sandburg

Get ready!

1 **Before you read the passage, talk about these questions.**

1 What are some different soil types?
2 What equipment digs deep into the ground?

Reading

2 **Read the letter from a contractor to a landowner. Then, mark the statements as true (T) or false (F).**

1 __ The topographic survey provides data for landscape design.
2 __ The preliminary investigation showed silt soil to be present.
3 __ The soil profile includes soil from twenty meters below the surface.

Vocabulary

3 **Match the words (1-6) with the definitions (A-F).**

1 __ sand
2 __ clay
3 __ gravel
4 __ surface evaluation
5 __ silt
6 __ topographic survey

A a soil type with particles measuring between 0.002 mm and 0.02 mm in diameter
B a soil type with particles measuring between 630 micrometers and 5 mm in diameter
C an examination of the top layer of soil at a construction site
D a soil type with particles measuring less than 0.002 mm in diameter
E a soil type with particles measuring between 5mm and 75mm in diameter
F an examination and description of the surface features of a construction site

4 Read the sentences and choose the correct words or phrases.

1 The contractor will need a **test pit / surface investigation** ten feet deep at this location.

2 Some soil will have to be moved to make this area **sand / level**.

3 Can that **test pit / drill rig** make a hole 25 meters deep?

4 Conduct a **subsurface investigation / topographic survey** to determine the foundation requirements.

5 The **drill rig / soil profile** shows a mix of clay and silt in this area.

5 🎧 **Listen and read the letter from a contractor to a landowner again. What does the surface evaluation consist of?**

Listening

6 🎧 **Listen to a conversation between a contractor and an employee. Choose the correct answers.**

1 What is the conversation mainly about?
- A why a drill rig is necessary
- B when clay soil might be dangerous
- C how to increase the strength of soil
- D what to do for a subsurface investigation

2 What will the woman do?
- A dig test pits
- B arrange a drill rig
- C obtain a soil profile
- D order stronger soil if needed

7 🎧 **Listen again and complete the conversation.**

Contractor:	Scott, **1** _____ _____ _____ to start that subsurface investigation tomorrow.
Employee:	Okay. What will be involved in that?
Contractor:	We need a **2** _____ _____ _____ . There's probably a good mix of soil types there.
Employee:	All right. **3** _____ _____ _____ _____ a drill rig?
Contractor:	**4** _____ _____ _____ . It's just for a house. Several small test pits should be fine.
Employee:	I see. **5** _____ _____ _____ should the test pits go?
Contractor:	Three or four meters **6** _____ _____ _____ .
Employee:	Got it. Anything else I should watch out for?
Contractor:	Knowing that area, there's probably some weak clay soil. Let me know if you come across any.

Speaking

8 With a partner, act out the roles below based on Task 7. Then, switch roles.

USE LANGUAGE SUCH AS:

I need you to ...
Should I ...?
Do you want me to ...?

Student A: You are a contractor. Talk to Student B about:
- a site investigation
- what is required for the investigation
- instructions for the investigation

Student B: You are an employee. Talk to Student A about a site investigation.

Writing

9 Use the letter and the conversation from Task 8 to complete the employee's notes.

Scott Carlson
Site Investigation Notes

Required: _____

_____

Not required: _____

_____

Watch out for: _____

_____

9

From: Jackie Sandburg
To: Luke Grissom
Re: Site Layout Today

Luke,

Today we'll finish the site layout for the office building on Lincoln Boulevard. We'll need to have a complete **site plan** by the end of the day. It should show the **property lines**, available **utilities**, and all significant changes in elevation.

I know this is your first time leading the crew. So I'll just give you a few reminders. Be sure your crew brings all the necessary equipment. Don't forget the **builder's level** and **grade rod**. You can't establish **horizontal** planes or measure elevation changes without them. There are already **bench marks** set at the site to help with that. You'll also need some **monuments** to **stake** out the property lines. Last, bring several **batter boards** and at least 100 meters of string or **wire**. Put the boards at the building corners. Then **run** the wire between them to show the wall outlines.

Jackie

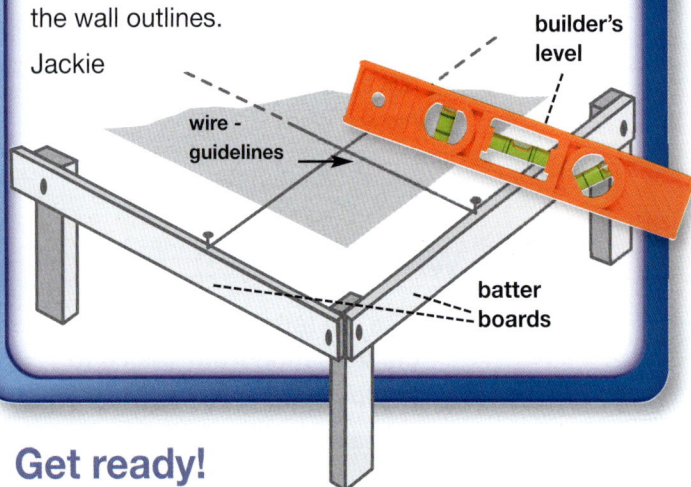

builder's level

wire - guidelines

batter boards

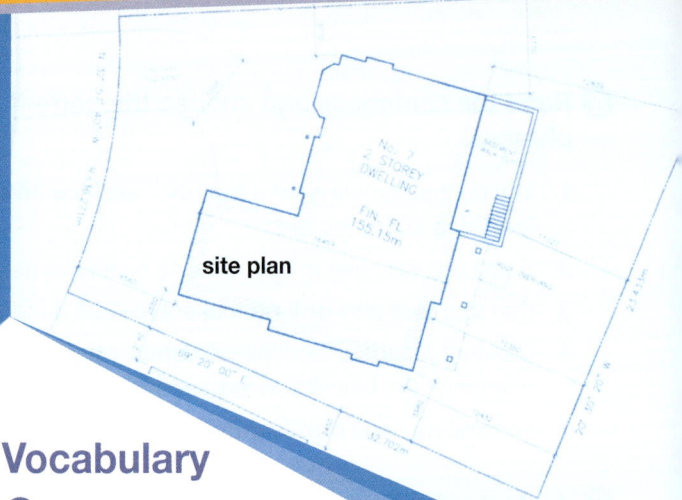

site plan

Get ready!

1 Before you read the passage, talk about these questions.

1 What is a map of a construction site called?

2 What is some equipment used for site layout?

Reading

2 Read the email from a contractor to a site manager. Then, mark the statements as true (T) or false (F).

1 __ The grade rod is needed to measure elevation changes.

2 __ The team has to set bench marks by the end of the day.

3 __ Batter boards and wire mark the property lines.

Vocabulary

3 Match the words (1-6) with the definitions (A-F).

1 __ site plan   4 __ utilities

2 __ horizontal   5 __ property line

3 __ batter board   6 __ wire

A a set of services required at most buildings, including electricity, natural gas, water, and sewage

B parallel to the plane of the horizon, or flat

C a drawing for a building project that shows its location, utilities, and property lines

D a piece of metal shaped into a thin, even thread

E a horizontal board fastened to a post and located at the corners of an excavation to mark the desired level

F the legal boundary of a piece of land owned by someone

4 Read the sentence pairs. Choose which word or phrase best fits each blank.

1 run / stake

A _____ the wire between the batter boards.

B Please _____ monuments at the corners of the property.

2 builder's level / grade rod

A A _____ is an optical instrument.

B This _____ has a target that corresponds to the instrument's line of sight.

3 bench mark / monument

A The _____ shows the elevation here.

B There is a _____ here showing the boundary of the property.

5 🎧 Listen and read the email from a contractor to a site manager again. What does the site plan need to show?

Listening

6 🎧 Listen to a conversation between a contractor and site foreman. Choose the correct answers.

1 What is the conversation mainly about?

  A correcting a mistake
  B meeting with a client
  C planning work for the day
  D locating necessary equipment

2 What task must be completed first?

  A setting up batter boards
  B staking the monuments
  C checking for elevation changes
  D running wire between batter boards

7 🎧 Listen again and complete the conversation.

Contractor: Well, there are several things that need to be done. Let's **1** _____ _____ staking the monuments.

Foreman: Will do. Should we run wire or string between batter boards **2** _____ _____ ?

Contractor: Oh, no. **3** _____ _____ .

Foreman: Really? We can't finish the site plan without them.

Contractor: That's true. We do need to plant the batter boards and run the wire. But we have to **4** _____ _____ _____ other business first.

Foreman: Oh, sorry. What should we **5** _____ _____ we stake the monuments?

Contractor: We should **6** _____ _____ elevation changes next.

Speaking

8 With a partner, act out the roles below based on Task 7. Then, switch roles.

Student A: You are a contractor. Talk to Student B about:

• a site layout
• what tasks need to be completed
• the order of events

Student B: You are a foreman. Talk to Student A about the plan for a site layout.

Writing

9 Use the email and the conversation from Task 8 to fill out the task sheet.

Task Sheet

Date: _____

Job: _____

Task 1: _____
Equipment/Items needed: _____
_____
_____

Task 2: _____
Equipment/Items needed: _____
_____
_____

Task 3: _____
Equipment/Items needed: _____
_____
_____

5 | Cranes

Martin & Martin
CRANE MANUFACTURING COMPANY

operator's cab

disassembly

stabilizer

Need a crane? Look no further than Martin and Martin Cranes. Whether you're building a multi-story home or a downtown skyscraper, we have what you need.

Martin and Martin manufacture a wide variety of cranes suitable for working on any building. We carry the finest and strongest **mobile cranes** and **stationary cranes**.

Need to work in multiple parts of a build site? Check out our new line of **crawler cranes** and **truck mounted cranes**.

For work on taller buildings, our **tower cranes** are unbeatable. And so is our service. We'll deliver and set up the crane. We provide the **stabilizers** and **outriggers** to **secure** your work and ensure your safety. All of our cranes are equipped with the highest standard of **operator's cabs**. Your operators will enjoy air conditioning and adjustable seats. And when the work is done, Martin and Martin's team of professionals perform all **disassembly** work.

tower crane

crawler crane

Get ready!

1 Before you read the passage, talk about these questions.

1 What type of crane is used to work on very tall buildings?

2 What happens when a crane's work is completed?

Reading

2 Read the manufacturer's brochure. Then, choose the correct answers.

1 What is the purpose of the passage?
  A to rate different crane companies
  B to advertise a construction company
  C to sell a company's services and cranes
  D to compare mobile cranes and tower cranes

2 What does the company NOT provide?
  A stabilizers   C crane operators
  B outriggers   D disassembly services

3 What can you infer about tower cranes?
  A They have multiple operator cabs.
  B They are smaller than crawler cranes.
  C They can move faster than truck cranes.
  D They cannot be transported in one piece.

Vocabulary

3 Match the words (1-6) with the definitions (A-F).

1 __ stabilizer   4 __ truck mounted crane
2 __ outrigger   5 __ crawler crane
3 __ mobile crane   6 __ stationary crane

A a mobile crane mounted on a truck
B a basic crane on a moveable platform
C a bracket that is attached to a crane
D a crane mounted on two moveable tracks
E a crane that does not move
F a mechanical device that helps keep a crane steady

4 Fill in the blanks with the correct words and phrases from the word bank.

word BANK

secure   operator's cab   disassembly   tower crane

1 A(n) _____ might be used to build a skyscraper.
2 The person who controls a crane sits in a(n) _____ .
3 The job is done, so we'll start _____ tomorrow.
4 Double check that equipment and _____ it carefully.

5 🎧 Listen and read the manufacturer's brochure again. What are the benefits of a crawler crane?

Listening

6 🎧 Listen to a conversation between a contractor and an employee. Choose the correct answers.

1 __ The woman is building a high-rise apartment complex.
2 __ The building will have a simple square design.
3 __ The man recommends a crawler crane.

7 🎧 Listen again and complete the conversation.

Contractor:	Hi, John. I'm a contractor with Olson Construction. I'd **1** _____ _____ _____ on selecting a crane.
Employee:	I can help you with that. What are you **2** _____ _____ ?
Contractor:	Well, we're building an apartment complex. But I'm not sure if we need a **3** _____ _____ _____ _____ .
Employee:	I see. It really depends on two things. First, is it a **4** _____ - _____ _____ ?
Contractor:	No, definitely not. It'll only be two stories.
Employee:	Okay, **5** _____ _____ _____ . And secondly, is it a basic design? Like a simple square?
Contractor:	No, **6** _____ _____ . There are a number of sections and offshoots.
Employee:	All right, then. From what I've heard, you don't want a tower crane.
Contractor:	Oh, no?
Employee:	Not with two stories and a complex design. I'd recommend a crawler crane.

Speaking

8 With a partner, act out the roles below based on Task 7. Then, switch roles.

USE LANGUAGE SUCH AS:

I'd like some advice ...
It depends on two things.
I'd recommend a ...

Student A: You are a crane company employee. Talk to Student B about:
• his or her project
• the building size and design
• the crane you recommend

Student B: You are a contractor. Talk to Student A about the best crane for a project.

Writing

9 Use the brochure and the conversation from Task 8 to fill out the call record.

Call Record

Employee: _____

Caller and company: _____

Calling about: _____

_____
_____

Project details: _____

_____
_____

Recommendation: _____

_____
_____

13

sling

wire rope sling

core

strand wire

strand

strand nicking

wire rope

chain sling

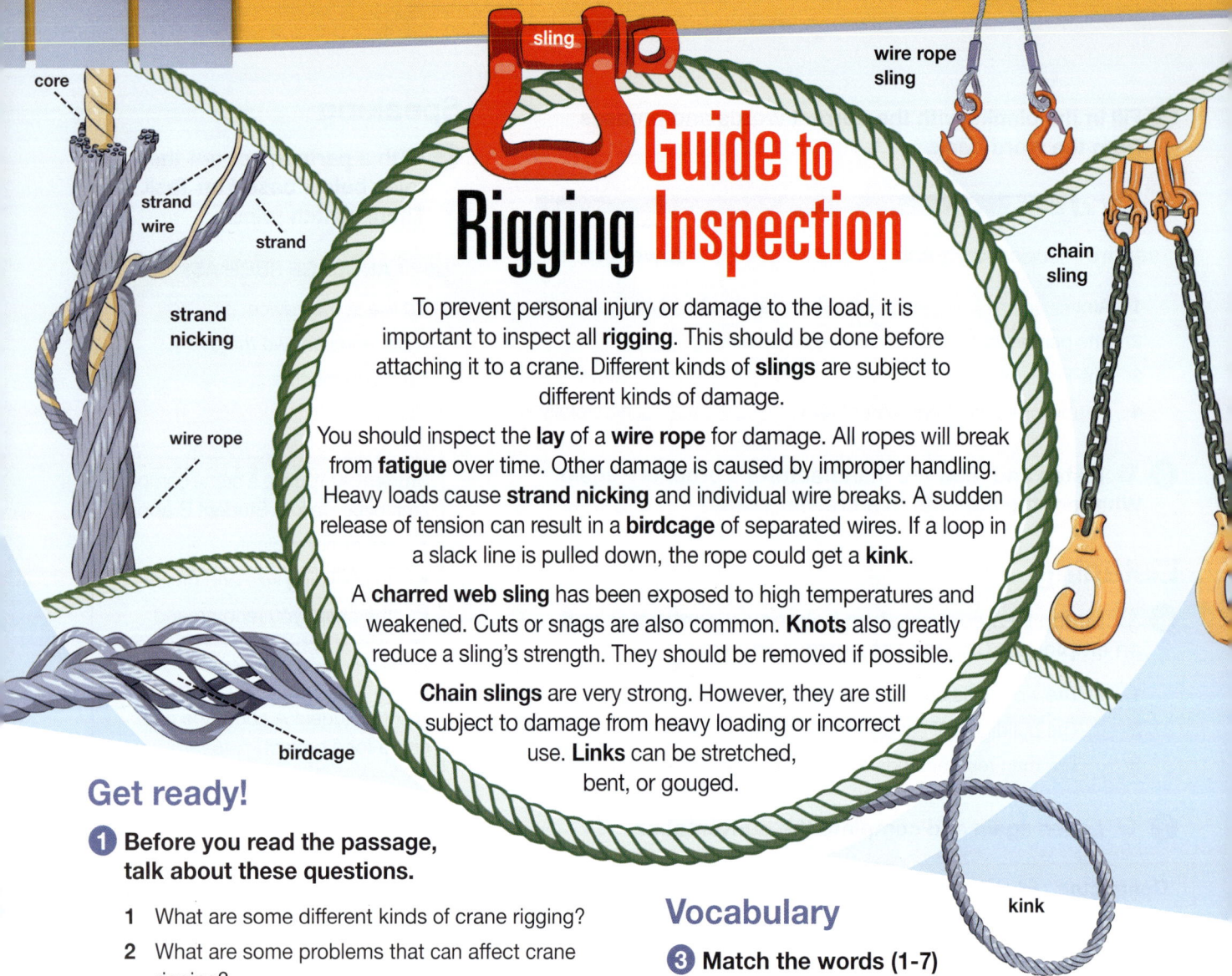

Guide to Rigging Inspection

To prevent personal injury or damage to the load, it is important to inspect all **rigging**. This should be done before attaching it to a crane. Different kinds of **slings** are subject to different kinds of damage.

You should inspect the **lay** of a **wire rope** for damage. All ropes will break from **fatigue** over time. Other damage is caused by improper handling. Heavy loads cause **strand nicking** and individual wire breaks. A sudden release of tension can result in a **birdcage** of separated wires. If a loop in a slack line is pulled down, the rope could get a **kink**.

A **charred web sling** has been exposed to high temperatures and weakened. Cuts or snags are also common. **Knots** also greatly reduce a sling's strength. They should be removed if possible.

Chain slings are very strong. However, they are still subject to damage from heavy loading or incorrect use. **Links** can be stretched, bent, or gouged.

birdcage

kink

Get ready!

1 Before you read the passage, talk about these questions.

1 What are some different kinds of crane rigging?
2 What are some problems that can affect crane rigging?

Reading

2 Read the instructions for inspecting rigging. Then, choose the correct answers.

1 What causes a birdcage in a wire rope?
   A normal fatigue
   B excessive heat
   C a release of tension
   D a pulled loop in a slack line

2 Which of the following is NOT a concern for web slings?
   A cuts   C burns
   B knots   D bent links

3 What kind of damage can occur to chain slings?
   A kinks   C gouged links
   B snags   D strand nicking

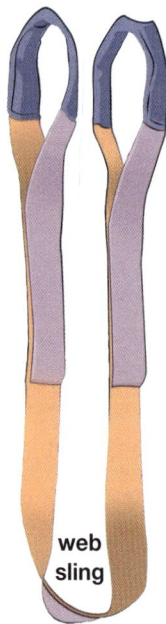

web sling

Vocabulary

3 Match the words (1-7) with the definitions (A-G).

1 __ fatigue   5 __ birdcage
2 __ kink   6 __ knot
3 __ web sling   7 __ lay
4 __ rigging

A the use of slings, ropes, and other equipment to move heavy objects with a crane

B a device made of nylon or polyester often used to lift objects in place of a wire rope

C a permanent distortion of wire strands caused when a loop in a slack rope is pulled down

D a looping of string or wire that cannot easily be untangled

E wear on a piece of equipment due to repeated use

F a length of rope equal to one spiral of a strand around the core

G a permanent separation of wire strands due to a sudden release of tension

4 **Read the sentence pairs. Choose which word or phrase best fits each blank.**

1 wire rope / sling

A This _____ has a kink and must be replaced.

B What kind of _____ should be used for this rigging?

2 strand nicking / charred

A This web sling was _____ by the fire.

B _____ happens when strands rub against each other.

3 chain sling / link

A She will need a _____ to lift this heavy load.

B Be sure to inspect each _____ for gouging.

5 🎧 **Listen and read the instructions for inspecting rigging again. What kinds of damage should you look for in a web sling?**

Listening

6 🎧 **Listen to a conversation between a construction worker and a manager. Mark the following statements as true (T) or false (F).**

1 __ The web sling can be repaired.

2 __ The man needs to lift an air conditioner.

3 __ The woman recommends using a wire rope.

7 🎧 **Listen again and complete the conversation.**

Worker:	I have a web sling here that is **1** _____ _____ .
Manager:	Really? **2** _____ _____ with it?
Worker:	I don't know how it happened. It has a pretty bad cut. It's definitely **3** _____ _____ _____ _____ .
Manager:	I see. I'm glad you spotted that. Do you have **4** _____ _____ you could use?
Worker:	There are a **5** _____ _____ _____ . I could go get a new web sling. Or, I could use a wire rope to lift the load instead.
Manager:	Hmm. What is the load?
Worker:	It's an air conditioning unit. It's going **6** _____ _____ _____ of the house.
Manager:	In that case, you'd better go get another web sling. We wouldn't want a wire rope to damage the unit.
Worker:	Sure thing. I'll be right back.

Speaking

8 **With a partner, act out the roles below based on Task 7. Then, switch roles.**

> **USE LANGUAGE SUCH AS:**
>
> *I have a ...*
> *What's wrong ...?*
> *I could ...*

Student A: You are a construction worker. Talk to Student B about:
- a problem with a sling
- options to replace the sling
- the right option to use

Student B: You are a manager. Talk to Student A about a problem with a sling.

Writing

9 **Use the instructions and the conversation from Task 8 to fill out the sling inspection report.**

JoS
Contractors

Sling Inspection Report

Problem: _____

_____

Options: _____

_____

Recommendation: _____

_____

15

excavation

pump

drill

runoff

●●● Water seepage

From:	Marcus-Adams@AdamsBuilders.com
To:	Randy-Walters@waltersconstruction.com
Subject:	Water seepage

Dear Randy,

I just wanted to let you know about a delay in construction.

We ran into a problem during today's **excavation**. While **drilling**, we encountered a large amount of seepage from **groundwater**. The **water table** in this area was unexpectedly high. Before we can proceed, we need to **extract** the water.

Since this isn't **runoff** or standing water, it won't be possible to let the water collect in a **sump**. The best way to solve this problem is by lowering the water level with a **dewatering system**. We will install a series of **well-points** throughout the area. As the water fills the well-points, we will use a **pump** to empty them. We will have to lower the water table by several feet.

I expect the process to take a few days. In the meantime, our crews will check the other areas of the construction site and make sure that this isn't a problem anywhere else.

If you have any questions, feel free to call me.
Marcus Adams

Get ready!

1 Before you read the passage, talk about these questions.

1 What is used to remove water from an area?

2 How do workers get through areas of hard rock?

Reading

2 Read the email from a contractor to a project manager. Then, mark the statements as true (T) or false (F).

1 __ The worksite was flooded by runoff.

2 __ The crew cannot use a sump to solve the problem.

3 __ Work cannot continue until the water table is lowered.

Vocabulary

3 Write a word that is similar in meaning to the underlined text.

1 We need to survey the area before <u>the process of digging holes into the ground</u> can begin.
   _ _ c a _ _ _ _ o _

2 Allow the liquid to enter the <u>reservoir that collects water</u> before you start to pump it.   _ u _ _

3 Because we got so much snow last winter, there is a high amount of <u>water flowing from land into rivers and streams</u> this spring.
   _ _ n _ f _

4 We can <u>forcibly remove</u> water from the ground using a pump.
   _ _ t _ _ c _

5 The <u>pipes that have been installed in the ground</u> allow water to flow in while keeping sand and rocks out.
   _ e _ _ - _ _ i n _ _

4 Fill in the blanks with the correct words and phrases from the word bank.

water table   groundwater   pump
drill   dewatering system

1 A _____ is a good way of lowering the underground water levels.

2 He attempted to _____ a hole in the ground, and hit a massive piece of rock.

3 The _____ rises and lowers according to environmental conditions, such as the amount of rainfall.

4 They used a _____ to collect the standing pool of water.

5 Most of our drinking supply comes from sources of _____ below the earth's surface.

5 🎧 Listen and read the email from a contractor to a project manager again. How does a dewatering system remove water?

Listening

6 🎧 Listen to a conversation between a construction worker and a project manager. Choose the correct answers.

1 What is the conversation mainly about?
   A a problem with a sump
   B why a new well-point is needed
   C how to remove water from a site
   D the success of a dewatering system

2 What will the woman most likely do next?
   A install a sump   **C** remove the well-point
   B begin construction   **D** replace the broken equipment

7 🎧 Listen again and complete the conversation.

Manager: **1** _____ _____ , Rachel?

Worker: Well, there's a huge pool of water where we **2** _____ _____ start building.

Manager: That's **3** _____ _____ . Is it standing water? Or do you think it's groundwater?

Worker: I'm **4** _____ _____ . The area around it seems to be dry.

Manager: Okay, well, let's **5** _____ _____ _____ it.

Worker: All right. **6** _____ _____ let it collect in a sump and then pump it out? Or start installing well-points?

Manager: Dewatering systems take a lot of time. We'd better go with the sump for now.

Speaking

8 With a partner, act out the roles below based on Task 7. Then, switch roles.

USE LANGUAGE SUCH AS:

We've got a problem.
Okay, well, let's ...
We'd better go with ...

Student A: You are a construction worker. Talk to Student B about:
• water that you have encountered on the excavation site
• methods of getting rid of the water

Student B: You are a project manager. Tell Student A how to get rid of the water.

Writing

9 Use the email and the conversation from Task 8 to fill out the manager's daily status report.

Excavation Project
Status Report

Today's task: _____
_____
_____

Problem: _____
_____
_____

Solution: _____
_____
_____

17

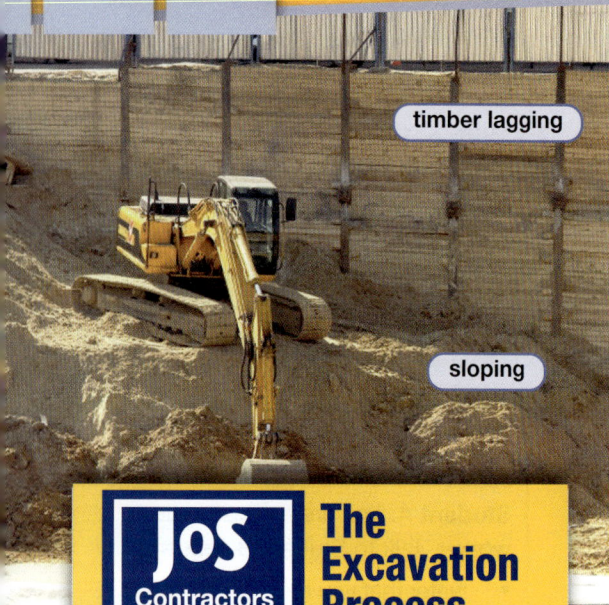

timber lagging

sloping

JoS Contractors

The Excavation Process

After your site is laid out, we will **dig** and remove earth for the foundation. Many jobs are **general excavations** that use standard machinery. Others may be **special excavations** requiring explosives or other equipment.

Please verify that the **payline** is marked accurately. This way we will only remove what is necessary. We will **haul** the earth and **deposit** it where you choose. Please note that **soil swell** can lead to more earth being hauled from that site. This can lead to additional charges for removal.

We will also talk to you about the best way to protect the dig site. The method selected depends on site conditions and project budget. Laying **timber lagging** between **steel soldier piles** is inexpensive and effective. **Interlocking sheet piling** creates a solid steel wall. If there is water nearby we may need to construct a **concrete slurry** wall. A **tieback** can protect a **sloping** excavation site while keeping it free of obstructions.

concrete slurry

Get ready!

1 **Before you read the passage, talk about these questions.**

1 What is another word for removing earth?

2 What is one way of protecting the dig site?

Reading

2 **Read the website from a construction company about excavation. Then, mark the statements as true (T) or false (F).**

1 __ General excavations usually require explosives.

2 __ Soil swell can increase hauling costs.

3 __ Timber lagging is used with interlocking sheet piling.

Vocabulary

3 **Match the words (1-7) with the definitions (A-G).**

1 __ dig   5 __ steel soldier piling

2 __ haul   6 __ deposit

3 __ sloping   7 __ concrete slurry

4 __ interlocking sheet piling

A running evenly upward or downward

B a method of supporting an earth wall using sheets of steel to form a single wall in the ground

C a material used to make protective excavation walls when the earth is very wet

D to remove earth from the ground

E sections of steel driven into the ground, used with timber sheeting to protect an excavation

F to carry something from one place to another

G to place something somewhere after it was moved from its original location

4 **Read the sentences and choose the correct words or phrases.**

1 The contractor will need to use explosives in this **special excavation / general excavation**.

2 Mark the **tieback / payline** correctly so the excavator doesn't remove more earth than we need.

3 Run some **timber lagging / concrete slurry** between those soldier piles to form a wall.

4 **Soil swell / Deposit** often leads to higher than expected hauling costs.

5 A **general excavation / special excavation** is one that can be completed using regular machines.

6 The subcontractor will use a **tieback / soil swell** here to keep the excavation area clear.

5 🎧 Listen and read the website from a construction company about excavation again. What will the site owner need to do during the process?

Listening

6 🎧 Listen to a conversation between two construction company managers. Choose the correct answers.

1 Why will a steel wall not work at the site?

   A There is not enough room.

   B The client cannot afford it.

   C It would not be strong enough.

   D The neighbors will not allow it.

2 What will the man likely do next?

   A send a report to the client

   B review the excavation plans

   C order the materials for a steel wall

   D call the neighboring property owners

7 🎧 Listen again and complete the conversation.

Manager 1:	Julie, have you looked over the plans for the Dobson property excavation?
Manager 2:	Yes, I was just checking them out. What are we going to use to protect and support the site?
Manager 1:	That's what I **1** _____ _____ _____ you about. Do you have any ideas?
Manager 2:	Well, a steel wall of interlocking **2** _____ _____ would be really strong.
Manager 1:	That **3** _____ _____ _____ . But, the fact is, we don't have enough space for that kind of wall.
Manager 2:	Hmm, I suppose you're right. **4** _____ _____ _____ a steel tieback system with a smaller wall inside?
Manager 1:	That might be possible. It would give us more **5** _____ _____ _____ .
Manager 2:	We'll have to **6** _____ _____ from the neighboring property owners. We'll need to place the ends of the tieback there.
Manager 1:	That could be a problem. I'll go give them a call.
Manager 2:	Sounds good. Let me know how it goes.

haul

Speaking

8 With a partner, act out the roles below based on Task 7. Then, switch roles.

> **USE LANGUAGE SUCH AS:**
>
> *That would be nice, but ...*
>
> *Could we use ...?*
>
> *We'll have to ...*

Student A: You are a construction company manager. Talk to Student B about:

- how to support an excavation site
- why one method will not work
- why another method may be better

Student B: You are a construction company manager. Talk to Student A about how to support an excavation site.

Writing

9 Use the website and the conversation from Task 8 to fill out the construction manager's notes.

JoS Contractors   Property Excavation

Support option 1: _____

_____

Problem: _____

_____

Support option 2: _____

_____

Problem: _____

_____

HOME | ABOUT US | SERVICES

stem wall

freeze

CENTURY Home Builders

The best homes last for generations. It all starts with the **foundation**. Century Home Builders is known for its sturdy **residential** structures.

CHB specializes in **shallow foundations**, including:

Monolithic foundations

In some areas, a monolithic foundation is the most stable option. The floor slab and the foundation are poured all at once. The foundation extends deeper below load bearing walls to support the **building load**.

Spread foundations

Century Home Builders provides spread foundations with **stem walls**. A wide **footing** is placed two feet below these walls. The stem walls rise above grade to protect structural walls from ground moisture and insects.

Foundation **piers** with **grade beams**

If you live on the coast, you're probably concerned about flooding. In that case, you'd want our foundation pier with grade beams. The grade beams support the load bearing walls, but also provide a crawl space below the house. When a flood occurs, it won't fill your first floor!

All CHB homes have our guarantee – they won't shift, crack, or settle when the ground **freezes** and **thaws**. CHB constructions are built to last!

residential

monolithic foundation

Get ready!

1 Before you read the passage, talk about these questions.

1 What is the bottom level of a building?

2 What is one condition caused by weather that could affect a foundation?

Reading

2 Read the website of a home-building company. Then, mark the statements as true (T) or false (F).

1 __ A monolithic foundation is created in several stages.

2 __ Stem walls rest on foundation piers.

3 __ Temperature changes in soil can potentially damage a foundation.

Vocabulary

3 Match the words (1-9) with the definitions (A-I).

1 __ footing
2 __ freeze
3 __ pier
4 __ residential
5 __ monolithic foundation
6 __ spread foundation
7 __ shallow foundation
8 __ grade beam
9 __ stem wall

A a foundation that distributes the weight from walls and columns over an area

B a concrete post that sits on piers and supports load bearing walls

C sections of concrete that lie below the foundation

D a foundation poured with a floor slab and with deeper parts below load bearing walls

E a concrete post formed by pouring concrete into a drilled hole

F a structure that rises above grade to which structural walls attach

G made up of many homes

H to become ice due to cold conditions

I a foundation that is constructed close to the surface

4 Read the sentences and choose the correct words or phrases.

1 These beams are not strong enough to support the **building load / footing** of the house.

2 The **building load / foundation** of the house cracked during the earthquake.

3 A **shallow foundation / grade beam** will not work for a high-rise building. It must go further into the ground.

4 The structure's foundation began to sink in the spring when all the ice **thawed / froze**.

5 🎧 Listen and read the website of a home-building company again. What are some advantages of a foundation pier with grade beams?

Listening

6 🎧 Listen to a conversation between a potential customer and a contractor. Choose the correct answers.

1 What is the conversation mainly about?
   - **A** how to install a foundation
   - **B** the pros and cons of different foundations
   - **C** why the man cannot use a certain foundation
   - **D** the cause of damage to the man's foundation

2 What does the man like about monolithic foundations?
   - **A** the price of installation
   - **B** the speed of installation
   - **C** the option for a crawl space
   - **D** the protection from flooding

7 🎧 Listen again and complete the conversation.

Customer:	Thanks for meeting with me again, Ms. Hendricks.
Contractor:	My pleasure. Now, have you thought about your foundation options?
Customer:	Well, I liked the monolithic foundation because it's **1** _____ .
Contractor:	It is the least expensive. It's also the **2** _____ _____ _____ , too. But there is a problem.
Customer:	Really? What's that?
Contractor:	This area **3** _____ _____ flood every few years. A monolithic foundation doesn't protect you from that.
Customer:	So what would you recommend?
Contractor:	Foundation piers with grade beams are **4** _____ _____ _____ . It lifts the house up a bit with a crawl space.
Customer:	I see. Are there any **5** _____ with that type?
Contractor:	A few. It **6** _____ _____ to install because we have to drill.

Speaking

8 With a partner, act out the roles below based on Task 7. Then, switch roles.

Student A: You are a potential home owner. Talk to Student B about:
- types of shallow foundations
- strengths of foundation types
- weaknesses of foundation types

Student B: You are a contractor. Talk to Student A about foundations.

Writing

9 Use the website and the conversation from Task 8 to fill out the information sheet from a construction company.

What you need to know about ...

Types of foundations

	Pros	Cons
Type 1 (Monolithic foundation)	_____	_____
Type 2 (Spread foundation with stem walls)	_____	_____

21

Get ready!

1 Before you read the passage, talk about these questions.

1 What machine puts piles into the ground?
2 What is one structure used with piles to support a foundation?

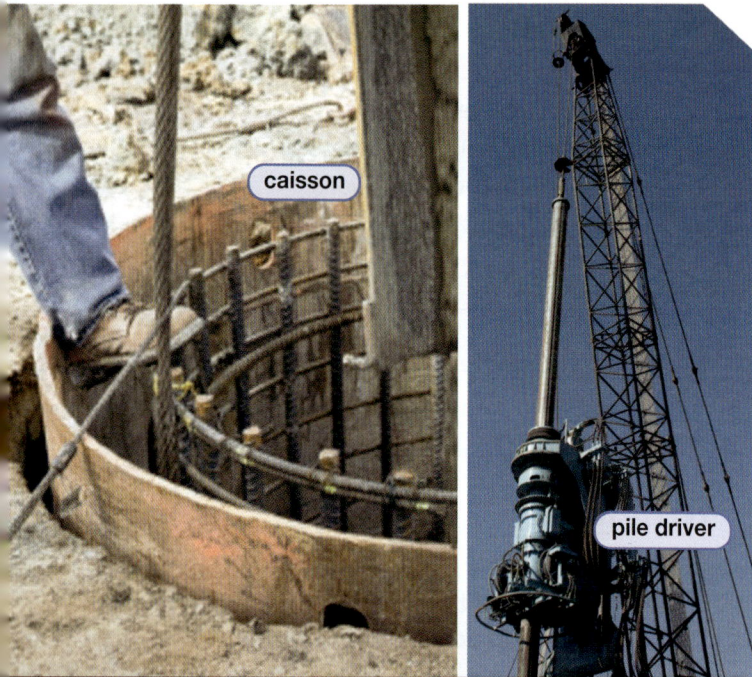

caisson

pile driver

Basic Construction Practices 334

Foundations and Piles

Foundations are one of the most essential parts of any building. Builders can use several different types of foundations and **piles**. The right kind depends on the design of the building and the type of soil.

For very heavy loads, it is best to put in a **deep foundation**. A **drilled foundation** with **cast-in-place piles** or a **driven foundation** with **bearing piles** is often a good choice. Workers use a **pile driver** to drive the piles into the ground. These deep foundations are suitable when bedrock can be reached. **Caissons** may also further support piles in a deep foundation.

If the soil contains more clay, then a **friction pile** or **friction plus bearing pile** is the best choice. However, horizontal pressure calls for another type of pile. For example, to hold up earth embankments, **sheet piles** are ideal.

Reading

2 Read the textbook entry. Then, mark the statements as true (T) or false (F).

1 __ Choosing a foundation depends on the type of soil.
2 __ Driven foundations cannot be used down to bedrock.
3 __ A bearing pile is best for soil with a lot of clay.

Vocabulary

3 Match the words (1-6) with the definitions (A-F).

1 __ cast-in-place piles   4 __ caissons
2 __ drilled foundation   5 __ friction pile
3 __ driven foundation   6 __ bearing pile

A a box that is filled with concrete
B a type of deep foundation in which piles are pushed into the ground
C a type of deep foundation formed by creating holes in the ground
D a pile that depends on frictional resistance between itself and the material it passes through.
E a pile with a large load capacity that transfers the weight of a load vertically
F a pile formed by pouring concrete into a drilled hole

4 Fill in the blanks with the correct words and phrases from the word bank.

wOrd BANK

piles   pile driver   deep foundation
friction plus bearing pile   sheet piles

1 A _____ is used to place piles in the ground.
2 A _____ goes all the way to bedrock.
3 Use _____ to hold up the embankment.
4 Jim ordered some concrete _____ for the new job.
5 A _____ should be used in soil with a lot of clay.

5 🎧 **Listen and read the textbook entry again. What types of foundations use piles?**

Listening

6 🎧 **Listen to a conversation between a teacher and a student. Choose the correct answers.**

1 What does the woman ask the man to do?

    A explain how to use pile drivers

    B compare the size of pile types

    C clarify the purpose of different piles

    D review the types of deep foundations

2 What does the man compare to a pile driver?

    A a drill   **C** a pipe

    B a hammer   **D** a nail

7 🎧 **Listen again and complete the conversation.**

Student: Mr. Olson? Last week in class you taught us about **1** ___ ___ _____ of foundations. Could I ask you a few questions?

Teacher: Of course, Lily. **2** _____ _____ .

Student: Well, you talked about deep foundations. I was a **3** _____ _____ about the different types.

Teacher: Okay. So a **4** _____ _____ is where deep holes are drilled into the ground. Then **5** _____ _____ are put in the holes.

Student: Wait, I thought that was a driven foundation. What's the difference?

Teacher: A **6** _____ _____ is a deep foundation, too. Piles are driven directly into the ground with a pile driver.

Speaking

8 **With a partner, act out the roles below based on Task 7. Then, switch roles.**

USE LANGUAGE SUCH AS:

I'm confused about ...

Wait, I thought that ...

Can I ask ... ?

Student A: You are a student. Talk to Student B about:

•   types of foundations

•   differences between two types

•   equipment used

Student B: You are a teacher. Talk to Student A about foundations.

Writing

9 **Use the textbook entry and the conversation from Task 8 to fill out the student's notes from class.**

Basic construction practices

notes

Student name: _____

Date: _____

Topic: _____

Two types of piles:

1. _____

   Used for: _____

2. _____

   Used for: _____

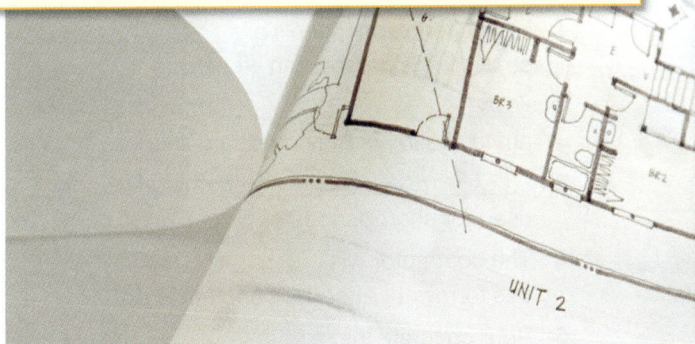

UNIT 2

11 Formwork 1

PXT FORMWORK

mold

formwork

framing

At PXT **Formwork** we specialize in the production of high-quality **prefabricated molds**.

These molds have steel or aluminum frames. The side facing the concrete is covered with the desired surface material. This may be steel or plywood. This type of formwork system is quick and easy to set up. The units are **lightweight** and easy to transport.

Prefabricated, **temporary** formwork molds are also easy to **strip** after the **consolidation** process. This occurs only after the concrete has **cured**. The beams are left behind until the structure has achieved its **design strength**. The concrete walls formed by these molds are capable of supporting any building's **framing**. The module frames can be **reused** thousands of times. You'll appreciate the time and money you save!

Our staff would be happy to provide a free consultation about your project's formwork needs. Contact us at service@pxtformwork.com to learn more about our products.

Get ready!

1 **Before you read the passage, talk about these questions.**

1   What kind of formwork is pre-made before arriving at a site?

2   What part of a building's structure are walls attached to?

Reading

2 **Read the advertisement for a formwork manufacturer. Then, mark the statements true (T) or false (F).**

1   __ The molds have frames made of plywood.

2   __ The formwork is difficult to strip.

3   __ The frames can be used many times.

Vocabulary

3 **Match the words (1-6) with the definitions (A-F).**

1   __ consolidation   4   __ framing

2   __ design strength   5   __ reuse

3   __ formwork   6   __ cure

A   to use something again

B   mold into which concrete or another material is poured to form a building structure

C   to dry until solid

D   the process of concrete becoming solid and denser, thereby taking up less space

E   the assumed load-bearing capacity of steel or concrete

F   the use of structural pieces to support a building and provide places to attach exterior and interior walls

4 **Fill in the blanks with the correct words from the word bank.**

WORD BANK

temporary   lightweight
mold   strip   prefabricated

1   Plastic formwork panels are _____, so even one person can lift them.

2   _____ formwork systems arrive already in the necessary shapes.

3   _____ formwork is only used for short periods of time.

4   The contractor will _____ this formwork after the concrete is dry.

5   Pour concrete into a _____ to shape it correctly.

24

5 🎧 Listen and read the advertisement for a formwork manufacturer again. What are the benefits of the company's temporary prefabricated molds?

Listening

6 🎧 Listen to a conversation between a project manager and a coworker. Choose the correct answers.

1 What is the current status of the building project?

    A Workers are pouring the concrete.

    B Workers are putting up the formwork.

    C They are waiting for the concrete to cure.

    D They are transporting the formwork to the site.

2 What will the woman likely do next?

    A drive to the job site

    B order more PTX molds

    C take the formwork to the site

    D remove the molds from the walls

7 🎧 Listen again and complete the conversation.

Coworker:	Oh yeah, I was wondering about that. How's it going?
Manager:	Really well, actually. We're using a new kind of concrete form.
Coworker:	The new PXT model? How's that **1** _____ _____ ?
Manager:	It's great. The modules are **2** _____ _____ . That makes them easy to set up and transport.
Coworker:	That's good. **3** _____ _____ _____ _____ on the project?
Manager:	We've poured the concrete. We **4** _____ _____ _____ for it to cure before taking the formwork down.
Coworker:	Of course. Those frames can be **5** _____ , right?
Manager:	Yes. With proper handling, the frames will **6** _____ _____ _____ .
Coworker:	Excellent. Keep me updated on the progress.

Speaking

8 With a partner, act out the roles below based on Task 7. Then, switch roles.

Student A: You are a project manager. Talk to Student B about:

• progress on a formwork project

• what kind of formwork is being used

• a benefit or drawback of using the formwork

Student B: You are the manager's coworker. Talk to Student A about progress on a formwork project.

Writing

9 Use the advertisement and the conversation from Task 8 to fill out the project progress update.

Project Progress Update

Project: _____

_____

Material used: _____

_____

_____

_____

_____

Current status: _____

_____

_____

_____

_____

_____

_____

_____

WOOD Formwork

How It Works

Several kinds of formwork are used in the construction industry today. The use of **modular systems**, **permanent insulated formwork**, and **stay-in-place** formwork is on the rise. However, the most common and affordable system remains wood formwork.

Wooden formwork is made of timber and **plywood**. It is assembled at the building site.

Wood can be used to make both **wall forms** and **footing forms**. Footing forms produce concrete columns and walls to serve as structure bases.

There are five essential parts to a wooden wall form. **Sheathing** lines the inside of the form to shape and hold the concrete. Vertical **studs** make a framework and support the sheathing. Horizontal **wales** serve to align the form and keep the studs in place. **Braces** help to keep the form standing up. Last, **tie-spreader units** maintain the correct spacing of the form. This basic structure has helped to erect buildings around the world.

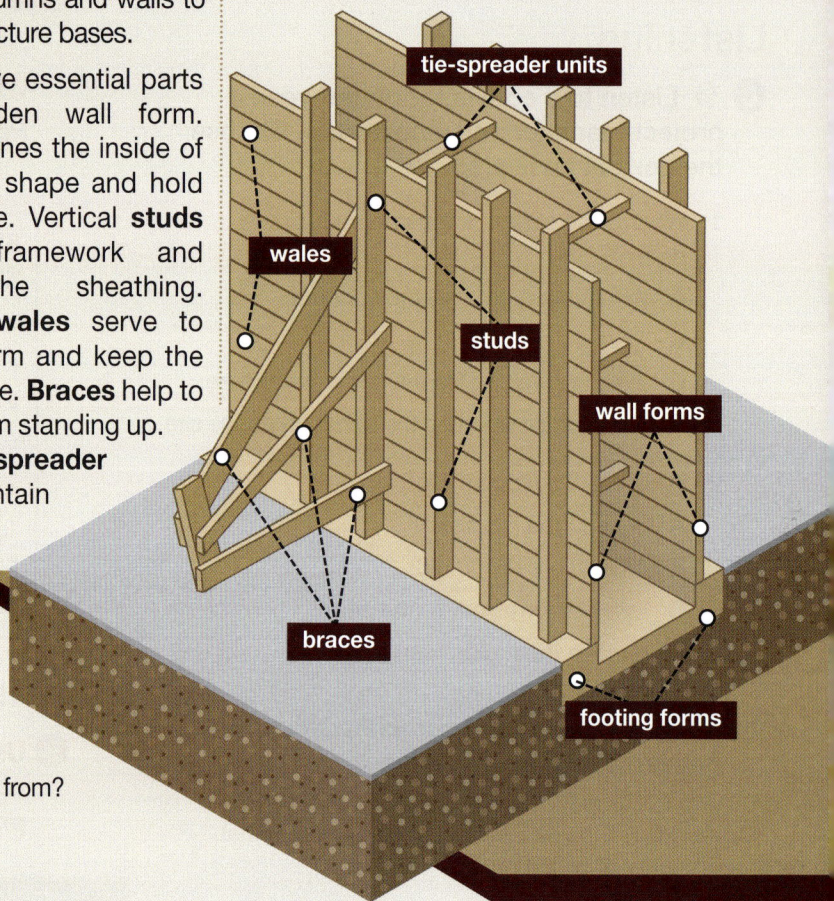

tie-spreader units
wales
studs
wall forms
braces
footing forms

Get ready!

1 Before you read the passage, talk about these questions.

1 What material is formwork commonly made from?

2 What part of a wooden formwork keeps it standing?

Reading

2 Read the article on wood formwork. Choose the correct answers.

1 What type of formwork is used most often?
   A wooden formwork
   B modular formwork
   C stay-in-place formwork
   D permanent insulated formwork

2 Which of the following is NOT part of a wall form?
   A braces   C tie-spreader unit
   B sheathing   D concrete column

3 What do wales do in a wall form?
   A hold the concrete
   B make the framework
   C maintain form spacing
   D keep the studs in position

Vocabulary

3 Match the words (1-6) with the definitions (A-F).

1 __ sheathing   4 __ tie-spreader unit
2 __ line   5 __ stay-in-place
3 __ wale   6 __ footing form

A a horizontal piece of lumber used to support or retain earth

B a device that holds the sides of a wall form at the correct spacing

C made from prefabricated plastic forms that remain after the concrete has cured

D a tube used to pour a concrete base column for a building structure

E something that wraps around or surrounds something else

F to cover the bottom or sides of something with a thin material

4 Read the sentence pairs. Choose which word or phrase best fits each blank.

1 **brace / stud**

   A Get a _____ to support this wall before it falls over.

   B The crew needs another _____ to complete this wall form.

2 **wall form / plywood**

   A This _____ is missing a brace.

   B Usually, wooden formwork is made from _____ .

3 **modular system / permanent insulated formwork**

   A This _____ will remain in place to give the structure added strength.

   B The contractor used a _____ made of aluminum sheets.

5 🎧 **Listen and read the article on wood formwork again. What are the parts of a wooden wall form?**

Listening

6 🎧 **Listen to a conversation between two construction workers. Mark the following statements as true (T) or false (F).**

1 __ The woman has not set up a plywood wall form before.

2 __ Braces are attached before wales.

3 __ The sheathing is attached after the tie-spreader units.

7 🎧 **Listen again and complete the conversation.**

Worker 2:	Okay. Could you **1** _____ _____ that process for me? It's my first time doing it.
Worker 1:	Sure. First, we'll **2** _____ _____ _____ _____ some studs with sheathing all along the wall form.
Worker 2:	Okay. That gives us the basic shape. **3** _____ _____ ?
Worker 1:	We'll put wales **4** _____ _____ _____ to support them.
Worker 2:	Wait a minute. Is that **5** _____ _____ _____ we attach braces?
Worker 1:	Before. The braces attach to the wales, so the wales have to **6** _____ _____ _____ .
Worker 2:	I see. And then we'll pour the concrete?
Worker 1:	Only after we've put in some tie-spreader units. That will keep the spacing right.
Worker 2:	I got it. It's not too complicated. I think I'm ready.

Speaking

8 With a partner, act out the roles below based on Task 7. Then, switch roles.

USE LANGUAGE SUCH AS:

Could you go over ...?

We'll need to ...

Is that before or after ...?

Student A: You are a construction worker. Talk to Student B about:

• the process for putting up formwork

• the correct order of steps

• correcting a mistake in order

Student B: You are a construction worker. Talk to Student A about the process for putting up formwork.

Writing

9 Use the article and the conversation from Task 8 to complete the wooden formwork instructions.

Setting Up
a Wooden Formwork

First step: _____

_____

Second step: _____

_____

Third step: _____

_____

Fourth step: _____

_____

13 Floor Plans

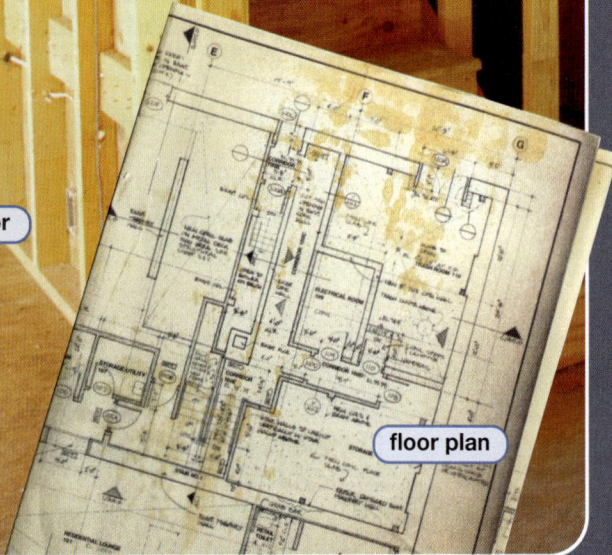

interior

floor plan

fixture

BUILDING PERMITS: FLOOR PLANS

What is a **floor plan**?

A floor plan is a detailed **diagram** of your proposed **building layout**. It describes the type of building as well as all major features. It is typically shown from a **bird's-eye view**. Every building project must submit a floor plan.

What must be included in a floor plan?

Every floor plan must **specify** the **dimensions** of the building and all **interior** rooms. The **function** of every room should be labeled. The **placement** of all **fixtures**, such as for plumbing and lighting, must be marked. Spaces for large **appliances** such as refrigerators are typically labeled as well. However, these labels are not required. Last, **indicate** nearby streets and utility access.

When do I submit a floor plan?

Submit a copy of your floor plan when your architect finalizes the design. The floor plan must be approved before you can begin excavation.

appliance

Get ready!

1 Before you read the passage, talk about these questions.

1 What is a detailed diagram of the inside of a building called?

2 Taps and sockets are examples of what?

Reading

2 Read the government website about building permits. Then, choose the correct answers.

1 What is the purpose of the website?

 A to demonstrate the layout of a floor plan

 B to explain requirements for floor plans

 C to help contractors submit floor plans

 D to describe the floor plan approval process

2 Which of the following does NOT have to be included in a floor plan?

 A the dimensions of the building

 B the placement of fixtures

 C the function of every room

 D the labels for appliance spaces

3 When should people submit a floor plan?

 A once they begin excavation

 B when the construction is finished

 C when the architect completes the design

 D after they have a first draft of the plan

Vocabulary

3 Match the words (1-6) with the definitions (A-F).

1 __ fixture   **4** __ building layout

2 __ interior   **5** __ indicate

3 __ specify   **6** __ bird's-eye view

A the inside part of a building or other structure

B showing a view from above

C a diagram drawn to scale showing the detailed features of an entire building

D a part of a building that is fixed in place and permanent

E to point something out or make it known

F to state or mark something clearly or in detail

4 Read the sentence pairs. Choose which word or phrase best fits each blank.

1 floor plan / function

   A The _____ of this fixture is not marked.

   B He needs to see the _____ of that office again.

2 dimensions / placement

   A The _____ of this room are not marked on the diagram.

   B Without the _____ of fixtures on the floor plan, we won't know where to install them.

3 diagram / appliance

   A This _____ is from a bird's-eye view.

   B It is not clear what kind of _____ this is in the kitchen.

5 🎧 Listen and read the government website about building permits again. What are some features that should be included in a floor plan submission?

Listening

6 🎧 Listen to a conversation between an architect and a contractor. Mark the following statements as true (T) or false (F).

1 ___ The woman calls about an error in the floor plan.

2 ___ The floor plan is for a new office building.

3 ___ The floor plan should not include appliance positions.

7 🎧 Listen again and complete the conversation.

Contractor:	I wanted to talk about the floor plan for the office we're building.
Architect:	I received your email earlier. We're just starting to **1** _____ _____ the floor plan.
Contractor:	That's great. Do you need any more **2** _____ ?
Architect:	**3** _____ _____ _____ _____ more about the purpose of the office?
Contractor:	It's a pretty standard **4** _____ _____ . It'll have a large room for desks and some offices along the walls.
Architect:	I see. **5** _____ _____ desks should fit in the large room?
Contractor:	The client wants **6** _____ _____ for fifteen.
Architect:	Okay. Should standard bathroom and break room fixtures be included?
Contractor:	Yes. There should be room for a full-size refrigerator in the break room.

Speaking

8 With a partner, act out the roles below based on Task 7. Then, switch roles.

USE LANGUAGE SUCH AS:

I wanted to talk to you about ...

Could you tell me ...?

It'll have a ...

Student A: You are an architect. Talk to Student B about:

- the floor plan for a new building
- what will be included
- appliances placement

Student B: You are a contractor. Talk to Student A about the floor plan for a new office.

Writing

9 Use the website and the conversation from Task 8 to fill out the floor plan design.

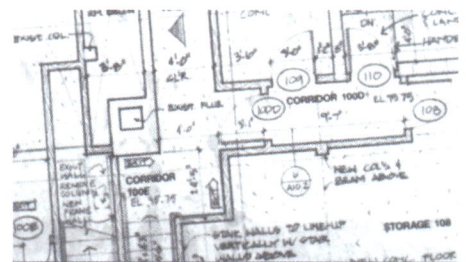

Glenn Associates

Floor Plan Design

Type of building: _____

_____

Space required: _____

_____

Fixtures and appliances: _____

_____

mudsill

floor

beam

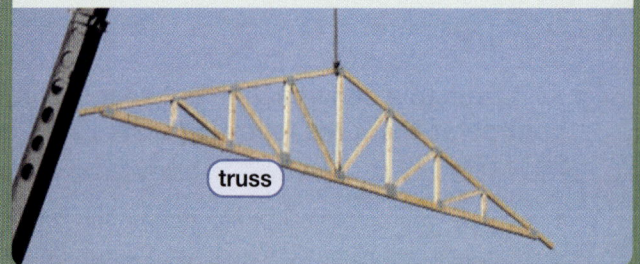

From: jim.martin@martinconstruction.com
To: bob.peterson@martinconstruction.com
Re: platform framing project

Mr. Peterson,

I'd like to discuss the **platform framing** project. Your last email mentioned that you are waiting for **joists** and **beams** to be delivered. When they arrive, go ahead and build the **support** for the **floor**. As a reminder, the beams need to be exactly six meters long. The joists should be placed apart and **parallel** to each other to **span** the floor.

Before you get started, please ensure that the **mudsills** and **joist connections** are in place and attached firmly. As we discussed, the wood used in this project should be hem-fir or spruce. These woods are a lot less expensive than oak. Also, ensure that the metal components of the **trusses** are approximately 20 cm in length. Once you've got the supports in place, go ahead and put in the **subfloor**. This will work as our **diaphragm**.

That's all for now. – Jim Martin

truss

Get ready!

1 Before you read the passage, talk about these questions.

1 What part of a frame provides support?

2 What is the name for a triangular structural frame?

Reading

2 Read the email. Then, choose the correct answers.

1 What is the purpose of the email?
   A to discuss the details of a project
   B to describe the mistakes on a project
   C to order some hem-fir wood beams
   D to give instructions about a subfloor

2 What information is NOT provided?
   A the length of the beams
   B the type of wood to use
   C the time of beam delivery
   D the span of the joists

3 What will happen after the beams arrive?
   A the subfloor will be replaced
   B the joist connections will be attached
   C the trusses will be measured
   D the support will be built

Vocabulary

3 Match the words (1-7) with the definitions (A-G).

1 __ subfloor   5 __ mudsill
2 __ support   6 __ truss
3 __ diaphragm   7 __ joist connection
4 __ joist

A a small piece of wood that connects the joists

B a piece of wood attached to a foundation that forms the base of a frame

C long structural frame made up of triangular shapes

D a structural plane designed to resist lateral force

E a series of wood beams that holds up a floor

F a layer of wood beneath the actual floor

G a piece of wood that spans the distance between beams

4 Fill in the blanks with the correct words from the word bank.

W O R D *BANK*

span   beam   floor   parallel

1 Use strong wood to _____ that gap.

2 The walls are _____ to one another.

3 A _____ supports all people and furniture in a building.

4 Don't use a _____ that has cracks or is bent.

5 🎧 Listen and read the email again. What are some types of wood that will be used in this floor?

Listening

6 🎧 Listen to a conversation between an employee and a supervisor. Choose the correct answers.

1 What problem do the speakers discuss?

   A the floor collapsed

   B the subfloor is too thin

   C the joist connections broke

   D the beams and joists are too small

2 What does the man suggest?

   A returning the old parts

   B building a new support

   C putting in a thicker subfloor

   D ordering new beams

7 🎧 Listen again and complete the conversation.

Supervisor:	Well, the joists and beams were **1** _____ _____ . They're **2** _____ _____ for that project. We're going to have to redo all of them.
Employee:	Isn't there something else we can do? Like **3** _____ _____ _____ thicker subfloor?
Supervisor:	No, it's too dangerous. The smaller beams can't **4** _____ _____ _____ . We have to replace them.
Employee:	That will be really expensive. We'll have to order brand new **5** _____ _____ _____ .
Supervisor:	I know, but it's a safety issue. The floor could collapse. So we **6** _____ _____ _____ it.

Speaking

8 With a partner, act out the roles below based on Task 7. Then, switch roles.

USE LANGUAGE SUCH AS:

There's a problem with the ...

The ... are too ...

The floor could collapse.

Student A: You are a supervisor. Talk to Student B about:

* a floor project

* a problem with some construction parts

* a solution

Student B: You are an employee. Talk to Student A about a problem with a floor project.

Writing

9 Use the email and the conversation from Task 8 to fill out the inspection report.

Inspection Report

Location: _____

Area inspected: _____

Problems: _____

_____

_____

Steps to be taken: _____

_____

_____

#Chapter 10

BASIC CONSTRUCTION PRACTICES

Concrete floors

Concrete floors are common in both single story buildings and **high-rises**. There are several different methods of arranging the **structural slabs** and support. It is important to be familiar with all types.

A standard **beam-and-slab** floor has concrete slabs supported by concrete beams. Beyond this, designs become more complex. A **one-way solid slab** floor has load-bearing steel running in the direction of the **span**. However, a **two-way solid slab** floor has load-bearing steel running in two directions. These are supported by concrete columns. Concrete **drop panels** are located in between the columns and the floor. A similar floor without drop panels is called a **two-way flat plate slab** floor. These are well-suited for **above grade** floors. Last, a **one-way joist slab** has a series of horizontal beams that contain reinforcing steel. These may be located at **construction joints**.

There are additional ways to reinforce a concrete floor. Running **tendons** through concrete, and then tightening and **anchoring** them after curing creates a strong **post-tensioned** floor. Also, a **cross-braced** floor, with diagonally intersecting supports, has increased **lateral stability**.

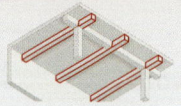
one-way solid slab

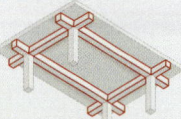
two-way solid slab

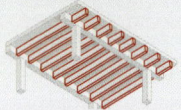
one-way joist slab

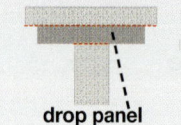
drop panel

two-way flat plate slab

high-rise

Get ready!

1 Before you read the passage, talk about these questions.

1 What are some structural supports for concrete floors?

2 What is another name for a skyscraper?

Reading

2 Read the textbook entry about concrete floors. Then, mark the statements as true (T) or false (F).

1 __ Load-bearing steel runs in the direction of the span in a one-way solid slab floor.

2 __ Drop panels are located in between concrete columns and a concrete floor.

3 __ Cross-braced floors are post-tensioned for added strength.

Vocabulary

3 Match the words (1-9) with the definitions (A-I).

1 __ two-way solid slab   6 __ span
2 __ one-way solid slab   7 __ drop panel
3 __ construction joint   8 __ post-tensioned
4 __ one-way joist slab   9 __ cross-braced
5 __ two-way flat plate slab

A a concrete surface where the laying of concrete was stopped and later continued

B concrete with tension added to it so that it can reach over a longer distance

C a structural slab with load-bearing steel running in the direction of the span and steel that controls cracking running perpendicular to the span

D the extent of a structure between supports

E a structural system that has a series of horizontal concrete beams containing reinforcing steel

F a thickened section of a concrete floor located over a supporting concrete column

G reinforced by diagonally intersecting supports

H a structural slab that has load-bearing steel running in two directions

I a structural slab similar to a two-way solid slab except that it does not have drop panels

4 Read the sentence pairs. Choose which word or phrase best fits each blank.

1 concrete floor / lateral stability

A This building is cross-braced for increased _____ .

B The _____ of this building is reinforced by steel beams.

2 high-rise / above grade

A This _____ building is over forty stories tall.

B The contractor is installing a floor _____ rather than underground.

3 tendon / beam-and-slab

A A strong _____ has been added to this concrete to give it tension.

B This _____ floor is a very common design.

⑤ 🎧 **Listen and read the textbook entry about concrete floors again. What are two ways to reinforce a concrete floor?**

Listening

⑥ 🎧 **Listen to a conversation between a contractor and an employee. Choose the correct answers.**

1 What is the conversation mainly about?

    A the concrete floor for a new project

    B the need for a stronger concrete floor

    C why a concrete floor is cracking

    D how to install drop panels from concrete floors

2 What is the benefit of a two-way flat plate slab floor?

    A It saves space.

    B It is less expensive.

    C It is faster to install.

    D It is stronger than other floors.

⑦ 🎧 **Listen again and complete the conversation.**

Contractor:	We're installing a concrete floor for the new **1** _____ _____ - _____ on Grant Avenue.
Employee:	**2** _____ _____ ! It sounds like a big project.
Contractor:	It is. I wanted to tell you about the **3** _____ _____ _____ we'll be putting in.
Employee:	I see. What's so special about it?
Contractor:	It's called a two-way **4** _____ _____ _____ floor.
Employee:	Hmm, I don't know **5** _____ _____ _____ exactly.
Contractor:	Well, it's supported by **6** _____ _____ . But you don't have to put drop panels between the columns and the floor.
Employee:	That's interesting. Sounds like that could save some space in a high-rise.

Speaking

⑧ **With a partner, act out the roles below based on Task 7. Then, switch roles.**

> **USE LANGUAGE SUCH AS:**
>
> *Let's talk a little about ...*
>
> *It sounds like ...*
>
> *It's a ...*

Student A: You are a contractor. Talk to Student B about:

- a new concrete floor project
- what kind of concrete floor is being used
- how the floor is supported

Student B: You are an employee. Talk to Student A about a new concrete floor project.

Writing

⑨ **Use the textbook entry and the conversation from Task 8 to fill out the new project plan.**

New Concrete Floor Project

Location: _____

Type of floor: _____

Support: _____

Glossary

4:1 rule [N-UNCOUNT-U2] The **4:1 rule** is a guideline which says that for every four feet of height a vertical surface has, a ladder must be one foot away from the surface.

above grade [ADJ-U15] If a part of a building is **above grade**, it is above ground level.

accident [N-COUNT-U2] An **accident** is an unexpected and undesired event, sometimes resulting in injury for the people involved.

anchor [V-T-U15] To **anchor** something is to hold it in a fixed place.

appliance [N-COUNT-U13] An **appliance** is an electrical device used in homes or offices to perform certain functions.

batter board [N-COUNT-U4] A **batter board** is a horizontal board fastened to a post and located at the corners of an excavation to mark the desired level.

beam [N-COUNT-U14] A **beam** is a long, heavy piece of wood.

beam-and-slab [N-UNCOUNT-U15] **Beam-and-slab** is a floor structure with concrete slabs supported by concrete beams.

bearing pile [N-COUNT-U10] A **bearing pile** is a pile with a large load capacity that transfers the weight of a load vertically.

bench mark [N-COUNT-U4] A **bench mark** is point of known elevation marked on a post or building near ground level.

birdcage [N-COUNT-U6] A **birdcage** is a permanent separation of wire strands due to a sudden release of tension.

bird's-eye view [N-PHRASE-U13] A **bird's-eye view** is a view from directly above.

brace [N-COUNT-U12] A **brace** is a piece of material used to transmit or change the direction of weight or pressure in a frame.

builder's level [N-COUNT-U4] A **builder's level** is an optical instrument that is used to establish or check points on a horizontal plane.

building layout [N-COUNT-U13] A **building layout** is a diagram drawn to scale showing the detailed features of an entire building.

building load [N-UNCOUNT-U9] A **building load** is the amount of force that a building must withstand, such as the weight of the structure itself, the weight of the items inside, and the forces of environmental factors, including wind and snow.

caisson [N-COUNT-U10] A **caisson** is a box that is filled with concrete and develops a form similar to a cast-in-place pile.

carpenter [N-COUNT-U1] A **carpenter** is a person trained to use wood to create buildings and other structures.

cast-in-place pile [N-COUNT-U10] A **cast-in-place pile** is a pile formed by pouring concrete into a drilled hole.

chain sling [N-COUNT-U6] A **chain sling** is a metal chain that is used to lift very heavy objects.

charred [ADJ-U6] If something is **charred**, it has dark marks and damage from being burned.

class [N-COUNT-U2] A **class** is a type of fire determined by fuel and causes.

clay [N-UNCOUNT-U3] **Clay** is a soil type with particles measuring less than 0.002 mm in diameter.

closed space [N-COUNT-U2] A **closed space** is an area that is indoors and sealed.

concrete floor [N-COUNT-U15] A **concrete floor** is a building floor made of concrete and supported by a structural frame.

concrete slurry [N-UNCOUNT-U8] **Concrete slurry** is a material used to make protective excavation walls when the earth is very wet.

consolidation [N-UNCOUNT-U11] **Consolidation** is the process of concrete becoming solid and denser, thereby taking up less space.

construction joint [N-COUNT-U15] A **construction joint** is a concrete surface where the laying of concrete was stopped and later continued.

contractor [N-COUNT-U1] A contractor is a person who performs specific tasks in the construction or improvement of a building, such as plumbing or electrical work.

core [N-COUNT-U6] The core is the central part of an object.

crawler crane [N-COUNT-U5] A crawler crane is a crane mounted on two moveable, motorized tracks.

cross-braced [ADJ-U15] If a building structure is cross-braced, it is reinforced by diagonally intersecting supports.

cure [V-I-U11] To cure is to dry until preserved, such as with concrete.

deep foundation [N-COUNT-U10] A deep foundation is a foundation that extends to bedrock.

deposit [V-T-U8] To deposit something is to place it somewhere.

design strength [N-UNCOUNT-U11] Design strength is the assumed load-bearing capacity of steel or concrete.

dewatering system [N-COUNT-U7] A dewatering system is a system in which a pump removes water from a series of well-points.

diagram [N-COUNT-U13] A diagram is a drawing that shows how something works or how parts fit together into a whole.

diaphragm [N-COUNT-U14] A diaphragm is a structural plane designed to resist lateral force.

dig [V-T-U6] To dig is to remove earth from the ground.

dimensions [N-PLURAL-U13] Dimensions are measurements of the amount of space something takes up, such as length, width, and height.

disassembly [N-UNCOUNT-U5] Disassembly is the process of taking things apart.

drill [V-T-U7] To drill is to make a hole in something.

drilled foundation [N-COUNT-U10] A drilled foundation is a type of deep foundation put in place with the use of drilling.

drill rig [N-COUNT-U3] A drill rig is a machine that digs a deep hole.

driven foundation [N-COUNT-U10] A driven foundation is a type of deep foundation where the piles are driven into the ground.

drop panel [N-COUNT-U15] A drop panel is a thickened section of a concrete floor located over a supporting concrete column.

electrician [N-COUNT-U1] An electrician is a person skilled in installing and repairing electrical equipment and wiring.

excavation [N-COUNT-U7] Excavation is the process of making a hole in the ground.

extract [V-T-U7] To extract something is to remove it.

fall [N-COUNT-U2] A fall is the act of hitting the ground from a higher position.

fatigue [N-UNCOUNT-U6] Fatigue is wear on a piece of equipment due to repeated use.

fixture [N-COUNT-U13] A fixture is a part of a building that is fixed in place, permanent, and performs a certain action.

floor [N-COUNT-U14] A floor is the bottom part of a room or building.

floor plan [N-COUNT-U13] A floor plan is a diagram drawn to scale showing the detailed features of one floor of a building.

footing [N-COUNT-U9] A footing is a structural implement that distributes the load of a building over the soil, over which the foundation is constructed.

footing form [N-COUNT-U12] A footing form is a tube used to pour a concrete base column for a building structure.

foreman [N-COUNT-U1] A foreman is a leader of a construction work crew.

formwork [N-UNCOUNT-U11] Formwork is a mold into which concrete or another material is poured to form a building structure.

foundation [N-COUNT-U9] A foundation is the underlying support for a structure, located below ground. It distributes the weight of the building onto the ground.

Glossary

framing [N-UNCOUNT-U11] Framing is the use of structural pieces to support a building and provide places to attach exterior and interior walls.

freeze [V-I-U9] To freeze is to turn into ice because of very cold conditions.

friction pile [N-COUNT-U10] A friction pile is a pile that depends on frictional resistance between itself and the material it passes through.

friction plus bearing pile [N-COUNT-U10] A friction plus bearing pile is a pile that depends on friction but also develops some end bearing.

function [N-COUNT-U13] A function is what something does or is used for.

general excavation [N-COUNT-U8] A general excavation is an excavation that includes work that can by done by mechanical equipment, such as shovels, scrapers, and trucks.

grade beam [N-COUNT-U9] A grade beam is a concrete post that sits on a pier and supports load bearing walls.

grade rod [N-COUNT-U4] A grade rod is a long wooden or aluminum staff used to determine differences in elevation.

gravel [N-UNCOUNT-U3] Gravel is a soil type with particles measuring between 5 mm and 75 mm in diameter.

ground [N-COUNT-U2] A ground is a device, typically a piece of wire or a metal rod, that is the return path for an electrical circuit. Sometimes grounds are connected to the earth.

groundwater [N-UNCOUNT-U7] Groundwater is a type of water located underground.

haul [V-T-U8] To haul something is to carry it from one place to another, often in a vehicle.

high-rise [N-COUNT-U15] A high-rise is a very tall building with many stories.

horizontal [ADJ-U4] If something is horizontal, it is parallel to the plane of the horizon, or flat.

HVAC technician [N-COUNT-U1] An HVAC technician is a person who is trained to install and repair heating, venting, and air conditioning systems.

indicate [V-T-U13] To indicate something is to point something out or make it known.

interior [N-COUNT-U13] An interior is the inside part of a building or other structure.

interlocking sheet piling [N-UNCOUNT-U8] Interlocking sheet piling is a method of supporting an earth wall using sheets of steel to form a single wall in the ground.

joist [N-COUNT-U14] A joist is a piece of lumber or wood that spans the distance between beams.

joist connection [N-COUNT-U14] A joist connection is a small piece of wood that connects the joists.

kink [N-COUNT-U6] A kink is a permanent distortion of wire strands caused when a loop in a slack rope is pulled down.

knot [N-COUNT-U6] A knot is a looping of string or wire that cannot easily be untangled.

laborer [N-COUNT-U1] A laborer is a person who uses physical strength and abilities to earn money.

ladder [N-COUNT-U2] A ladder is a portable device that has steps, called rungs, which a person can use to climb up and down a vertical surface.

lateral stability [N-UNCOUNT-U15] Lateral stability is the ability of a structure to resist movement from side to side.

lay [N-COUNT-U6] A lay is a length of rope equal to one spiral of a strand around the core.

level [ADJ-U3] If something is level, it is flat or at the same height in all places.

lightweight [ADJ-U11] If something is lightweight, it does not weigh very much.

line [V-T-U12] To line something is to cover its inner surface with something else.

link [N-COUNT-U6] A link is a single piece of metal chain.

mason [N-COUNT-U1] A mason is a person who builds structures with stone or brick.

Material Safety Data Sheet [N-COUNT-U2] A Material Safety Data Sheet is a document that gives essential information about a substance, including how to handle it, where to store and dispose of it, what hazards are associated with it, and how to treat an exposure to the substance.

mobile crane [N-COUNT-U5] A mobile crane is a basic crane mounted on a moveable platform.

modular system [N-COUNT-U12] A modular system is a formwork system consisting of prefabricated sheets of steel, aluminum, or plastic that are joined together on site.

mold [N-COUNT-U11] A mold is a hollow form for shaping a fluid substance, such as wet concrete.

monolithic foundation [N-COUNT-U9] A monolithic foundation is a foundation in which the floor slab and foundation are poured at the same time. The foundation extends deeper at the load bearing walls.

monument [N-COUNT-U4] A monument is a marker that establishes the boundary of a piece of property.

mudsill [N-COUNT-U14] A mudsill is a piece of wood attached to a foundation and forms the base of a wood frame.

one-way joist slab [N-COUNT-U15] A one-way joint slab is a structural system that has a series of horizontal concrete beams containing reinforcing steel.

one-way solid slab [N-COUNT-U15] A one-way solid slab is a structural slab with load-bearing steel running in the direction of the span and steel that controls cracking running perpendicular to the span.

operator's cab [N-COUNT-U5] An operator's cab is a small enclosure where a person sits and operates a crane.

outrigger [N-COUNT-U5] An outrigger is a bracket that is attached to a crane to add stability.

painter [N-COUNT-U1] A painter is a person who paints surfaces (indoor or outdoor) with a paintbrush or other equipment.

parallel [ADJ-U14] If two things are parallel, they extend in the same direction.

payline [N-COUNT-U8] A payline is a line in the ground surrounding the material for which an excavation contractor is paid to remove.

permanent insulated formwork [N-UNCOUNT-U12] Permanent insulated formwork is a formwork system consisting of concrete forms that remain after the concrete has cured.

pier [N-COUNT-U9] A pier is a concrete post created by filling a drilled hole with concrete. The pier is used to support beams in a foundation.

pile [N-COUNT-U10] A pile is a weight-bearing pole made of wood, steel or concrete.

pile driver [N-COUNT-U10] A pile driver is a machine designed to drive piles into the ground.

placement [N-COUNT-U13] A placement is the location or position of something.

platform framing [N-UNCOUNT-U14] Platform framing is a type of floor construction using levels.

plywood [N-UNCOUNT-U12] Plywood is a manufactured lumber made from thin sheets of wood glued together.

post-tensioned [ADJ-U15] If concrete is post-tensioned, it has steel tendons running through it, which are tightened after the concrete cures to provide additional strength.

prefabricated [ADJ-U11] If something is prefabricated, it is manufactured in a standard format, with final assembly at the building site.

property line [N-COUNT-U4] A property line is the legal boundary of a piece of land owned by someone.

pump [N-COUNT-U7] A pump is a machine that transfers liquids and gases into and out of an area.

pump jack [N-COUNT-U2] A pump jack is a platform that can be raised or lowered by pumping a device up and down.

residential [ADJ-U9] If an area is residential, it consists mainly of houses, rather than buildings for businesses.

reuse [V-T-U11] To reuse something is to use it again.

rigging [N-UNCOUNT-U6] Rigging is the slings, ropes, and other equipment used to move heavy objects with a crane.

roofer [N-COUNT-U1] A roofer is a person who lays and repairs the roofs of buildings.

run [V-T-U4] To run something is to extend it over a certain distance.

runoff [N-UNCOUNT-U7] Runoff is water that flows from land into rivers, streams, and other bodies of water.

sand [N-UNCOUNT-U3] Sand is a soil type with particles measuring between 630 micrometers and 5 mm in diameter.

Glossary

scaffold [N-COUNT-U2] A scaffold is a raised platform that workers stand on.

secure [V-T-U5] To secure something is to prevent it from moving.

semiskilled [ADJ-U1] If a worker is semiskilled, he or she is partially trained or experienced, but is not fully skilled.

shallow foundation [N-COUNT-U9] A shallow foundation is a foundation that distributes a building load relatively close to the surface. This type is commonly used for private homes.

sheathing [N-UNCOUNT-U12] Sheathing is something that wraps around or surrounds something else.

sheet pile [N-COUNT-U10] A sheet pile is a pile intended to withstand horizontal pressure.

silt [N-UNCOUNT-U3] Silt is a soil type with particles measuring between 0.002 mm and 0.02 mm in diameter.

site plan [N-COUNT-U4] A site plan is a drawing for a building project that shows its location, utilities, and property lines.

skilled [ADJ-U1] If a worker is skilled, he or she has special abilities or training for a job.

sling [N-COUNT-U6] A sling is the part of rigging that attaches the load being lifted to the crane.

sloping [ADJ-U8] If a surface is sloping, it runs evenly upward or downward.

soil profile [N-COUNT-U3] A soil profile is a description of the variation of soil types at a construction site.

soil swell [N-UNCOUNT-U8] Soil swell is the increase in soil volume after it is excavated and no longer compacted.

span [V-I-U14] To span something is to reach across it.

span [N-COUNT-U15] A span is the distance or gap between supports.

special excavation [N-COUNT-U8] A special excavation is an excavation that includes work done by blasting, hand, or special machines.

specify [V-T-U13] To specify something is to state or mark it clearly or in detail.

spread foundation [N-COUNT-U9] A spread foundation is a foundation that distributes the weight of the heaviest parts of a structure over a large area to ensure that the load does not surpass the location's bearing capacity.

stabilizer [N-COUNT-U5] A stabilizer is a mechanical device that helps keep a crane steady and still.

stake [V-T-U4] To stake a pole or marker is to drive it into the ground.

stationary crane [N-COUNT-U5] A stationary crane is a crane that does not move.

stay-in-place [ADJ-U12] If a formwork system is stay-in-place, it is made from prefabricated plastic forms that remain after the concrete has cured.

steel soldier piles [N-COUNT-U8] Steel soldier piles are sections of steel driven into the ground, used with timber sheeting to protect an excavation.

stem wall [N-COUNT-U9] A stem wall is a part of a spread foundation that rises slightly above the ground. The structural wall attaches to the stem wall.

strand nicking [N-UNCOUNT-U6] Strand nicking is damage to a wire rope caused by strands rubbing against each other.

strip [V-T-U11] To strip a formwork mold is to remove it.

structural slab [N-COUNT-U15] A structural slab is a large piece of concrete that is a component of a concrete floor.

stud [N-COUNT-U12] A stud is a vertical post used in construction, often made of wood.

subcontractor [N-COUNT-U1] A subcontractor is a worker for a specific purpose at a construction site who is hired by the general contractor rather than the customer.

subfloor [N-COUNT-U14] A subfloor is a layer of wood beneath the actual floor.

subsurface investigation [N-COUNT-U3] A subsurface investigation is an examination of the soil beneath the surface at a construction site to establish what is required for the foundation of the structure.

sump [N-COUNT-U7] A sump is a chamber where water collects before a pump removes it.

support [N-COUNT-U14] A support is a series of wood beams that holds up a floor.

surface evaluation [N-COUNT-U3] A surface evaluation is an examination of the top layer of soil at a construction site, primarily to establish drainage grades and landscaping requirements.

temporary [ADJ-U11] If something is temporary, it is not permanent.

tendon [N-COUNT-U15] A tendon is a high-strength steel strand used to add tension to concrete.

test pit [N-COUNT-U3] A test pit is a hole dug at a construction site in order to obtain soil samples.

thaw [V-I-U9] To thaw is to melt through exposure to warmth.

tieback [N-COUNT-U8] A tieback is a system for externally bracing an excavation in order to provide an unobstructed excavation area.

tie-spreader unit [N-COUNT-U12] A tie-spreader unit is a device that holds the sides of a wall form at the correct spacing.

timber lagging [N-UNCOUNT-U8] Timber lagging is a set of wooden planks placed between steel soldier piles to protect an excavation.

topographic survey [N-COUNT-U3] A topographic survey is an examination and description of the surface features of a construction site.

tower crane [N-COUNT-U5] A tower crane is a very tall type of stationary crane.

toxic [ADJ-U2] If a substance is toxic, it is poisonous.

trench safety [N-UNCOUNT-U2] Trench safety is the practice of taking proper safety precautions when working in trenches.

truck mounted crane [N-COUNT-U5] A truck mounted crane is a mobile crane mounted on the back of a truck.

truss [N-COUNT-U14] A truss is a long structural frame made up of triangular shapes.

two-way flat plate slab [N-COUNT-U15] A two-way flat plate slab is a structural slab with load bearing steel running in two directions, and that does not have drop panels.

two-way solid slab [N-COUNT-U15] A two-way solid slab is a structural slab that has load-bearing steel running in two directions.

unskilled [ADJ-U1] If a worker is unskilled, he or she does not have any special training for a job.

utilities [N-PLURAL-U4] Utilities are a set of services provided to most buildings, including electricity, natural gas, water, and sewage.

ventilation [N-UNCOUNT-U2] Ventilation is the circulation of fresh air in a room or structure.

wale [N-COUNT-U12] A wale is a horizontal piece of lumber used to support or retain earth.

wall form [N-COUNT-U12] A wall form is the complete structure used to build a wall, consisting of sheathing, studs, wales, braces, and tie spreaders.

water table [N-COUNT-U7] The water table is the level in the ground where the ground is fully saturated with groundwater.

web sling [N-COUNT-U6] A web sling is a device made of nylon or polyester often used to lift objects in place of a wire rope.

well-point [N-COUNT-U7] A well-point is a pipe that is put in the ground. It has holes through which water enters the pipe to be pumped out.

wire [N-COUNT-U4] A wire is a piece of metal shaped into a thin, even thread.

wire rope [N-COUNT-U6] A wire rope is a rope made of thin pieces of metal wire twisted around a core.

CAREER PATHS

Construction I
Buildings

Book
3

Virginia Evans
Jenny Dooley
Jason Revels

Express Publishing

Scope and Sequence

Unit	Topic	Reading context	Vocabulary	Function
1	Prints 1	Email	complex, cross section, elevation, horizontally, irregular, isometric drawing, oblique drawing, orthographic projection, plan view, section, sketch, vertically	Introducing a problem
2	Prints 2	Textbook	architect's scale, centerline, cutting-plane line, dimension line, extension line, hidden line, leader, object line, scale, scale drawing	Asking for clarification
3	Concrete Work 1	Webpage	aggregate, air entrainment, bind, cement paste, coarse aggregate, concrete, fine aggregate, heavyweight concrete, insulating concrete, lightweight concrete, normal-weight concrete, set, shrink, void	Correcting an assumption
4	Concrete Work 2	Website	air content test, cleanliness, collapse, colorimetric test, gradation, moisture test, organic impurity, shear, silt test, slump test, soundness, specific gravity, true slump, water:cement ratio	Changing the subject
5	Concrete Work 3	Website	belt conveyor, bucket, buggy, chute, countercurrent mixer, drum mixer, finish, float, mixing, place, screed, strike off, trowel, uniformity, wheelbarrow	Emphasizing a point
6	Timber Frames	Construction manual	dead load, deflection, glued-laminated timber, glulam rivet, live load, pin-type connection, shear plate, split-ring connector, timber connectors, transfer, truss plate timber	Describing uses
7	Steel Frames	Safety guidelines	anchor bolt, ASTM designation, bearing plate, bearing-type connection, bolting, column, erection mark, fillet weld, friction-type connection, gauge, girder, groove weld, member, open-web steel joist, pitch, section shape, steel frame	Confirming details
8	Concrete Frames	Website	brittle, concrete frame, coupler, cover, lap splice, mechanical splice, precast, prestressed, reinforcement, splice, tensile strength, welded splice, welded wire reinforcement, wire mesh	Stating an opinion
9	Doors and Windows	Product descriptions	automatic door, awning, bifold door, casement, double-hung, fire door, fixed, frame sash, hopper, pane, pocket door, revolving door, sliding	Describing options
10	Insulation	Work order	asbestos, batt, building envelope, glass wool blanket, insulating concrete form (ICF),insulation, loose fill, natural fiber, R-value, rigid panel, spray polyurethane foam (SPF), vapor retarder	Expressing doubt
11	Stairs	Instructions	baluster, balustrade, banister, flight, going, landing, newel, nosing, riser, riser height, spandrel,stairs, stringer, tread, tread depth	Making an apology
12	Masonry	Advertisement	bearing wall, cavity wall, curtain wall, grout, mason, masonry, masonry unit, mortar, multiwythe, single wythe, veneer	Describing benefits
13	Roofs 1	Article	drain, elements, flashing, gravel stop, gutter, parapet, rain, roof, roof deck, roof frame, roof membrane, scupper, slope, snow, vapor barrier, walk	Giving assurances
14	Roofs 2	Advertisement	eave, flat roof, gable, gambrel, hip, low slope roof, mansard, purlin, rafter, rake, shake, shed, shingle, vent	Describing attributes
15	Finishing	Email	cladding, cornice, drop ceiling, exterior finishing,finish, install, interior finishing, painting, partition, plaster, siding, tile, trim	Discussing options

Table of Contents

Get ready!

1 Before you read the passage, talk about these questions.

1 What is another name for a 3-D drawing of a building?

2 What view shows a building's height?

isometric drawing

cross section

elevation view

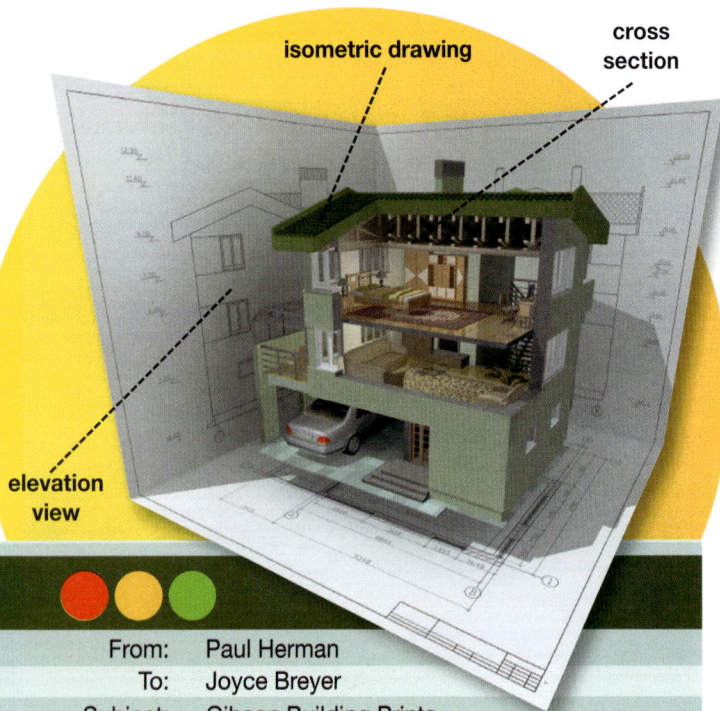

From: Paul Herman
To: Joyce Breyer
Subject: Gibson Building Prints

Hi Joyce,

I wanted to update you on my progress on the prints for the Gibson building.

I completed the **orthographic projection** of the building's exterior. This includes a **plan view** of the roof and **elevations** of all sides. I also completed **section** views of several interior walls. This will let you easily see where plumbing and other fixtures should be installed.

The prints of the building's interior sections are not yet finished. I have completed **isometric drawings** of several rooms. These prints produce three dimensional images because lines are drawn at thirty degree angles instead of **horizontally**. Unfortunately, I am having trouble drawing some of the **irregular** wall features, such as moldings. The best way to show these is in **oblique drawings**. They have the most **complex** surface flat against the paper. This is a time-consuming process, but I am working as quickly as I can. For additional detail, I am also including some **cross sections** of these surfaces. For your reference, these will be **vertically** oriented.

I attached a rough **sketch** of the building layout. Please look it over and let me know if you have any questions or concerns.

Thanks,
Paul

Reading

2 Read the email from an architect to a contractor. Then, choose the correct answers.

1 What is the purpose of the email?

   A to correct an error in the building prints

   B to list what types of prints need to be created

   C to explain why orthographic projections are not needed

   D to inform the contractor of what prints are complete and incomplete

2 Which of the drawings are NOT finished?

   A plan views   C oblique drawings

   B section views   D building layout sketch

3 Why is the architect struggling with some drawings?

   A Several surfaces have been redesigned.

   B Some wall features have complex surfaces.

   C He has to show where plumbing fixtures are installed.

   D He does not have accurate elevation measurements.

Vocabulary

3 Match the words (1-6) with the definitions (A-F).

1 __ cross section   4 __ irregular

2 __ isometric drawing   5 __ plan view

3 __ orthographic projection 6 __ complex

A a type of drawing that separates each side of an object and shows it flat as if projected against the side of a glass box

B a construction drawing with objects shown in three dimensions by drawing horizontal lines at a 30 degree angle

C made up of many parts or very detailed

D the point where a two-dimensional plane intersects with a three-dimensional object, as shown in a section drawing

E a construction drawing shown from above

F not having many straight, geometric lines

4 Fill in the blanks with the correct words and phrases from the word bank.

WORD BANK

section   oblique drawing   vertically
elevation   horizontally   sketch

1 A floor plan is really a(n) _____ view with the roof cut off.

2 Mark the elevation _____ on this drawing.

3 Please draw a rough _____ of the building plan.

4 A(n) _____ is useful to show an object with an irregular side.

5 Draw that line _____ , from left to right.

6 This drawing shows the _____ of the building from ground to roof.

5 🎧 Listen and read the email from an architect to a contractor again. What exterior drawings has the architect done?

Listening

6 🎧 Listen to a conversation between a contractor and an architect. Mark the following statements as true (T) or false (F).

1 __ The woman calls to make an appointment to review the prints.

2 __ The measurements in two drawings do not match.

3 __ The man cannot complete the woman's request.

7 🎧 Listen again and complete the conversation.

Contractor: Hi Paul, this is Joyce Breyer. I was just **1** _____ _____ the prints that you sent over yesterday.

Architect: Great. How do they look?

Contractor: Generally they look great. There's **2** _____ _____ _____ .

Architect: Oh, really? What's that?

Contractor: Well, in the plan view you labeled the front office as measuring ten meters by twelve meters.

Architect: Right, I remember that.

Contractor: But here's the problem. In the **3** _____ _____ it's ten meters by fifteen meters.

Architect: Oh my, I'm glad you **4** _____ _____ .

Contractor: I think it's **5** _____ _____ _____ ten by twelve.

Architect: I think you're right. I'll double check **6** _____ _____ to be sure.

Contractor: Okay. Can you get me a copy of the corrected print today?

Speaking

8 With a partner, act out the roles below based on Task 7. Then, switch roles.

USE LANGUAGE SUCH AS:

I was just looking over ...
I think it's supposed to be ...
Can you get me ...?

Student A: You are a contractor. Talk to Student B about:
- building prints you received
- a problem with one of the prints
- when the new prints will be sent

Student B: You are an architect. Talk to Student A about building prints.

Writing

9 Use the email and the conversation from Task 8 to write a report on the building prints. Write about:
- when they were sent
- any errors
- when the next draft will arrive

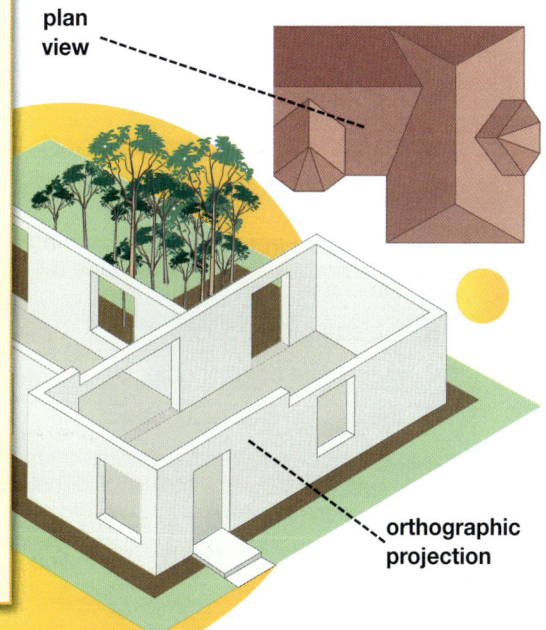

plan view

orthographic projection

5

Scale drawings and lines

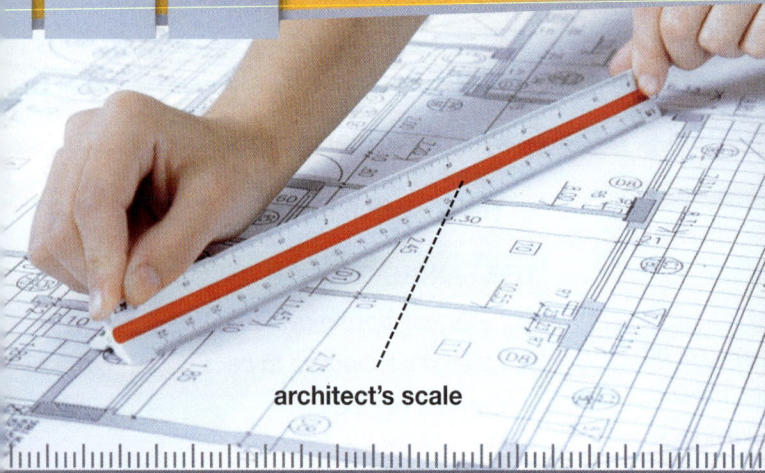

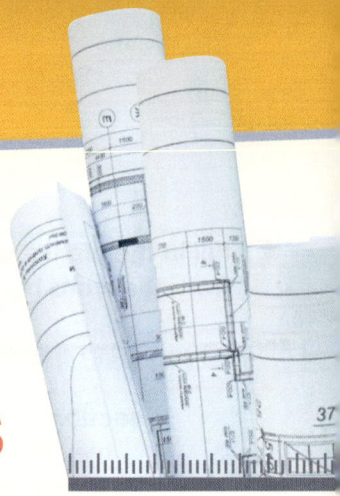

architect's scale

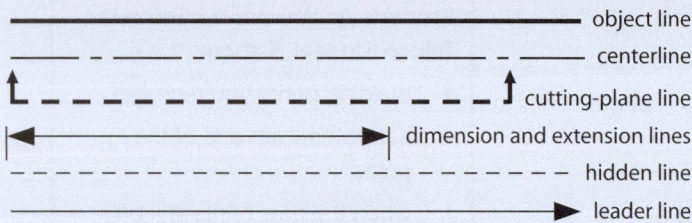

object line
centerline
cutting-plane line
dimension and extension lines
hidden line
leader line

Every construction worker must know how to read a **scale drawing**. These illustrations show the layout for a construction project in an accurate **scale**. Construction drawings are made using an **architect's scale**, which often has two scales on one face. You may not be required to use this instrument. However, you should recognize the multiple types of lines that drafters make on drawings.

The most basic line is the **object line**. It is a heavy, solid line that shows the shape of an object.

If the side of an object would not normally be seen, a dashed line called a **hidden line** represents it.

Extension lines and **dimension lines** are thin, solid lines. They show the size of an object, such as its length or width. A short extension line extends out from each side of the object. A dimension line connects the two extension lines, with the measurement written above it.

You will see a few other lines on drawings. A **centerline** with long and short dashes shows the center axis of an object. A thin line with an arrow called a **leader** labels objects and dimensions in tight spaces. A **cutting-plane line** shows where an imaginary cut was made to obtain a section-view drawing.

Get ready!

1 **Before you read the passage, talk about these questions.**

1 What instrument does an architect use to measure scale?

2 What are some types of lines in construction drawings?

Reading

2 **Read the textbook entry on construction drawings. Then, choose the correct answers.**

1 What should every construction worker be able to do?
   A make scale drawings
   B use an architect's scale
   C identify drafting line mistakes
   D recognize different kinds of drafting lines

2 What does a hidden line show?
   A the shape of an object
   B the size of an object
   C the middle point of objects
   D the unseen side of an object

3 Which of the following is NOT a solid line?
   A extension line   C object line
   B centerline   D dimension line

Vocabulary

3 **Match the words (1-5) with the definitions (A-E).**

1 __ dimension line   4 __ hidden line
2 __ object line   5 __ leader
3 __ cutting-plane line

A a line in a drawing that indicates where a section view is taken from and in what direction it is viewed

B a line in a drawing that connects an object with its label

C a line in a drawing that shows edges that are hidden from normal view

D a line in a drawing that shows the size, such as length or width, of an object

E a solid line in a drawing that shows the shape of an object

4 Fill in the blanks with the correct words and phrases from the word bank.

scale   extension line   centerline
architect's scale   scale drawing

1   Use the _____ to complete the drawing.
2   A(n) _____ shows the middle of an object.
3   The print has a(n) _____ of 100 to 1.
4   The architect is still creating the _____ .
5   This _____ connects to the dimension line to make the drawing clearer.

5 🎧 Listen and read the textbook entry on construction drawings again. How are object lines and hidden lines related?

Listening

6 🎧 Listen to a conversation between a student and an instructor. Mark the following statements as true (T) or false (F).

1   ___ The man is confused about two types of lines.
2   ___ A cutting-plane line shows a center axis.
3   ___ Cutting-plane lines are always solid.

7 🎧 Listen again and complete the conversation.

Student:	I'm having trouble understanding the **1** _____ _____ some types of drafting lines.
Instructor:	They can be tricky to **2** _____ _____ . Which ones are confusing you?
Student:	A centerline and a **3** _____ - _____ _____ . Don't they both show the center of something?
Instructor:	Not necessarily. You're right that a centerline shows the **4** _____ _____ of something.
Student:	Okay. But doesn't a cutting-plane line show **5** _____ _____ _____ ?
Instructor:	No. It shows where the cut for a **6** _____ _____ _____ is. That doesn't have to be in the middle of the object.
Student:	Oh, I see. It doesn't have to divide the object in half.
Instructor:	That's right. You can also tell them apart by how they look.
Student:	A cutting-plane line is usually solid, right?
Instructor:	It can be either solid or dashed. And a centerline has long and short dashes.

Speaking

8 With a partner, act out the roles below based on Task 7. Then, switch roles.

USE LANGUAGE SUCH AS:

I'm having trouble understanding ...
Don't they both ...
You can also tell them apart ...

Student A: You are a student. Talk to Student B about:
• a question on drafting lines
• the different purposes of the lines
• how to tell the lines apart

Student B: You are an instructor. Talk to Student A about a question on drafting lines.

Writing

9 Use the textbook entry and the conversation from Task 8 to write the student's notes. Write about:
• what some lines do
• how each is written

7

3 Concrete Work 1

HOME   ABOUT US   SERVICES   CONTACT

ABOUT US

ABC Cement and **Concrete** is a family-owned business. We have been operating from the same location for nearly four decades. Our company provides a full range of services for all your concrete needs.

Our concrete starts with the finest quality cement and water. We then add the **cement paste** to the right blend and size of **aggregate**. Our attention to the mixing process ensures that each concrete blend is perfect. It doesn't matter if you're looking for **normal-weight concrete**, **lightweight concrete**, **insulating concrete**, or **heavyweight concrete**. We can provide exactly what you need.

We offer a wide range of **fine aggregate** and **coarse aggregate**. They ensure that your concrete **binds** correctly. This way, you can custom design the perfect concrete for you and your building project. We even provide **air entrainment** to most types of concrete. The additional voids it creates help your concrete **set** perfectly and prevent it from **shrinking**. Combined with steel rebars, our concrete can support almost any load.

ABC Cement and Concrete can work with you on-site or deliver pre-mixed batches. We'll meet your needs. So come in to ABC Cement and Concrete for the region's best service and highest quality concrete.

cement paste   fine aggregate

coarse aggregate   shrink

Get ready!

1 Before you read the passage, talk about these questions.

1 What two components along with water make up concrete?

2 What is one problem that can affect concrete?

Reading

2 Read the webpage. Then, choose the correct answers.

1 What is the purpose of the page?

   A to provide instructions for mixing concrete

   B to describe a concrete company's services

   C to inform contractors about concrete prices

   D to explain the differences between types of concrete

2 What ensures the concrete binds correctly?

   A air   **B** cement   **C** aggregates   **D** steel rebar

3 Why does the company perform air entrainment?

   A to ensure proper binding

   B to prevent concrete from setting

   C to decrease the number of voids

   D to avoid any concrete shrinking

Vocabulary

3 Match the words (1-8) with the definitions (A-H).

1 __ concrete   4 __ set   7 __ bind

2 __ shrink   5 __ void   8 __ air entrainment

3 __ aggregate   6 __ cement paste

A to attach something to something else

B the act of mixing small bubbles into concrete

C a mixture of cement, water, and aggregate

D to become hard and solid

E a gap in a substance

F a material that helps bind cement

G to become smaller

H the substance formed when water and cement combine

4 Fill in the blanks with the correct words and phrases: *lightweight concrete*, *normal-weight concrete*, *coarse aggregate*, *insulating concrete*, *fine aggregate*, *heavyweight concrete*.

1 _____ should never be used to support a load. It is only used to control temperature.

2 Large stones or chunks of rock are examples of _____ .

3 _____ is the densest type of concrete.

4 Sand is a common _____ .

5 _____ is the least dense type of concrete that can still support a load.

6 _____ is denser than the lightest concrete, but still lighter than the heaviest types of concrete.

5 🎧 Listen and read the webpage again. How can contractors prevent concrete from breaking or shrinking?

Listening

6 🎧 Listen to a conversation between a contractor and an employee. Mark the following statements as true (T) or false (F).

1 ___ The man is confused because the concrete won't set.

2 ___ The man thinks heavyweight concrete is the best choice.

3 ___ The woman wants to use sand as an aggregate.

7 🎧 Listen again and complete the conversation.

Employee:	Excuse me, Ms. Brown. Could I **1** _____ _____ _____ ?
Contractor:	Of course, Sam. What's going on? Is there **2** _____ _____ ?
Employee:	Well, not really. I'm just a little bit confused about something. I just **3** _____ _____ _____ it with you.
Contractor:	Sure. Has the concrete set too slowly again?
Employee:	No, no. That's fine. We fixed **4** _____ _____ .
Contractor:	Good. So what's your question?
Employee:	It's about the type of concrete we're using. Are we using **5** _____ _____ ?
Contractor:	Yes, we are.
Employee:	Right. This is a really **6** _____ _____ , so shouldn't we use heavyweight concrete?
Contractor:	No, lightweight is fine.
Employee:	I thought that **7** _____ _____ wasn't strong enough.
Contractor:	I see why you are asking. Actually, though, that's not the case.
Employee:	It isn't?
Contractor:	No. Lightweight concrete is suitable as long as it has **8** _____ _____ _____ .
Employee:	Oh. So, we'll use pumice as an aggregate, I assume.
Contractor:	No, that's not correct. We need to go with a coarse aggregate, like gravel.

Speaking

8 With a partner, act out the roles below based on Task 7. Then, switch roles.

Student A: You work for a contractor. Talk to Student B about:

• the type of concrete to use

• a concern about the concrete

• the type of aggregate to use

Student B: You are a contractor. Talk to Student A about concrete.

Writing

9 Use the webpage and the conversation from Task 8 to create a pamphlet for a concrete manufacturer. Write about:

• the types of concrete offered

• how it is made

• the aggregate used

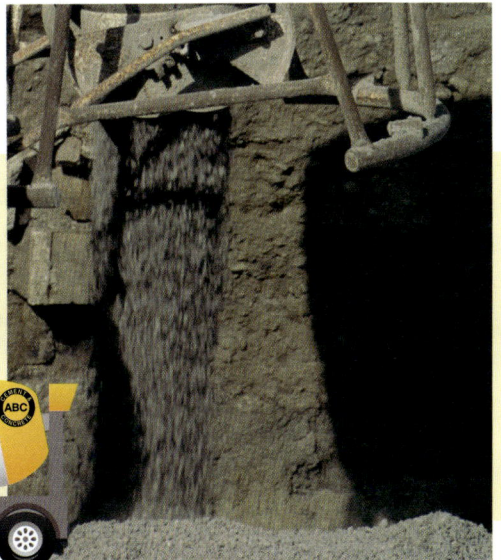

Concrete Work 2

JPX Concrete Testing

JPX Concrete Testing offers a variety of tests for concrete during all stages of the construction process. Our staff will come to your worksite to conduct tests and collect samples. We pride ourselves in providing fast and reliable results. Our most common tests include:

Test	What It Measures
Soundness	The strength of aggregate used in concrete mixes.
Silt Test	The **cleanliness** of coarse aggregate. Too much fine material can make the aggregate unusable.
Colorimetric Test	The presence of **organic impurities** in fine aggregate. Too many make the aggregate unusable.
Gradation	The distribution of particle size in aggregate. A mix of large and small is desirable.
Slump Test	The flowability of a concrete mix. A **true slump** retains its shape when tested, while a **collapse** or **shear** breaks apart. Such slumps often mean the mix is too wet.
Moisture Test	The amount of water in an aggregate. A high amount of moisture may require a lower **water:cement ratio** to produce a strong mix.
Air Content Test	The amount of air in a concrete mix. Some air is often desired to help concrete flow.
Specific Gravity	The ratio of an aggregate's mass to the mass of an equal volume of water.

true slump

Loss of strength

SPECIFIED SLUMP

50% INCREASE IN SLUMP

100% INCREASE IN SLUMP

200% INCREASE IN SLUMP

| ADDITIONAL WATER | none | +10L/m³ [5%] | +20L/m³ [10%] | +30L/m³ [15%] |

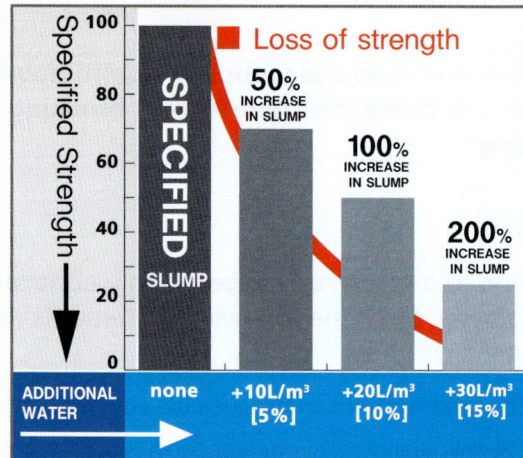

water:cement ratio	
m³	kg
Cement	Water
1 kg/m³	200 kgr

Clay layer- water clears
Silt layers- 2 hours
Sand layers- 1 minute

silt test

Get ready!

1 Before you read the passage, talk about these questions.

1 What are some different types of concrete tests?

2 What test separates sand, silt, and clay layers?

Reading

2 Read the website from a concrete testing company. Then, mark the following statements as true (T) or false (F).

1 __ A colorimetric test looks for organic impurities in coarse aggregate.

2 __ Aggregate particles should be about the same size.

3 __ The water:cement ratio should decrease when there is a lot of moisture in the aggregate.

Vocabulary

3 Match the words (1-8) with the definitions (A-H).

1 __ silt test   5 __ specific gravity

2 __ slump test   6 __ soundness

3 __ cleanliness   7 __ colorimetric test

4 __ shear   8 __ gradation

A a test to determine the presence of fine organic matter in fine aggregate

B a kind of concrete slump in which the top portion of the concrete breaks off and slips sideways

C a measurement of the strength of an aggregate used in a concrete mix

D a test to measure how easily a concrete mix flows

E the distribution of particle sizes in the aggregate used in a concrete mix

F a test to determine the presence of very fine material in a coarse aggregate

G the ratio of something's mass to the mass of an equal volume of water.

H a measurement of the presence of silt and other matter sticking to coarse aggregate used in a concrete mix

4 Read the sentence pairs. Choose which word or phrase best fits each blank.

1 organic impurity / true slump

   A A colorimetric test will show if there is a(n) _____ in this aggregate.

   B A(n) _____ is desired for the best workable concrete.

2 water:cement ratio / air content test

   A The _____ showed an acceptable amount of air in this concrete mix.

   B The _____ of this mix needs to be increased.

3 moisture test / collapse

   A Please conduct a _____ on this aggregate.

   B This slump _____ means that the mix is too wet.

5 🎧 Listen and read the website from a concrete testing company again. What does a slump test show?

Listening

6 🎧 Listen to a conversation between a concrete tester and a contractor. Choose the correct answers.

1 What is the conversation mainly about?

   A the cause of organic impurities

   B the type of aggregate to use in a mix

   C good and bad results of aggregate tests

   D how to achieve the proper water:cement ratio

2 Which test did the aggregate fail?

   A silt test   **C** colorimetric test

   B gradation test   **D** moisture content test

7 🎧 Listen again and complete the conversation.

Contractor:	Good to know. What else?
Tester:	It has an adequate moisture content. That means we won't have to adjust the **1** _____ _____ in the mix.
Contractor:	Good. Doing that **2** _____ _____ sometimes.
Tester:	Right. Now, on to the **3** _____ _____ . Unfortunately, the aggregate failed the silt test.
Contractor:	**4** _____ _____ , what does that mean?
Tester:	There's a lot of **5** _____ _____ _____ mixed in with the aggregate. We'd have to use more paste to cover it all.
Contractor:	Of course. Is there anything we can do about it?
Tester:	We can try to remove some of the material. It should be do-able but it means more **6** _____ _____ _____ .

Speaking

8 With a partner, act out the roles below based on Task 7. Then, switch roles.

USE LANGUAGE SUCH AS:

It passed the ...

Now, on to the ...

We can try to ...

Student A: You are a concrete tester. Talk to Student B about:

- the results of concrete tests
- which tests were passed
- a test that was failed

Student B: You are a contractor. Talk to Student A about the results of concrete tests.

Writing

9 Use the website and the conversation from Task 8 to write a concrete test report. Write about:

- 3 different tests

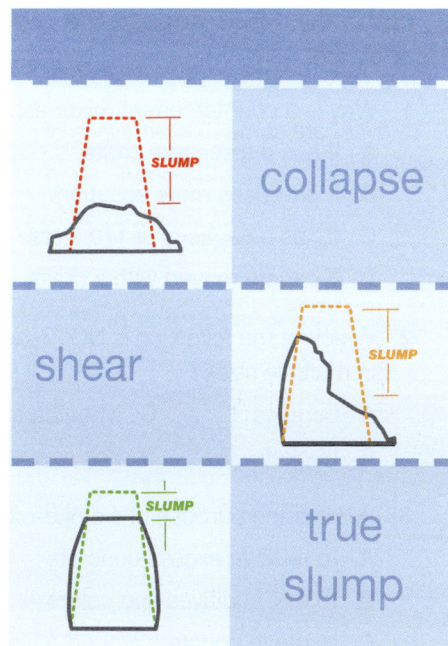

SLUMP

collapse

shear

SLUMP

SLUMP

true slump

wheelbarrow

HOME ABOUT US SERVICES CONTACT

MVJ Construction Supply

Concrete equipment

MVJ Construction Supply can provide your company with everything it needs for concrete projects. We have equipment for every step of the process.

drum mixer

belt conveyor

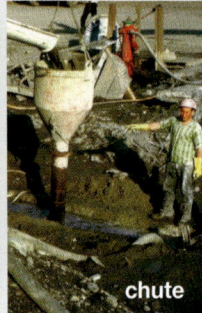
chute

Mixing

Drum Mixers: These mixers are available in sizes from 0.10 cubic meters to 1.5 cubic meters. They either tilt to unload or have a discharge **chute**.

Countercurrent Mixers: These mixers create more agitation than a drum mixer for greater **uniformity**. They are especially useful when mixing additives and colors.

Transport

Wheelbarrows: The average capacity of our wheelbarrows is 170 liters. Smaller and larger sizes are available.

Buggies: Both our pushcarts and motorized buggies have pressurized tires for easy, smooth operation. Their capacity ranges from 0.10 to 0.30 cubic meters.

Buckets: We stock many kinds of buckets, from small hand-held buckets to large crane-lifted containers.

Belt Conveyor: Portable belt conveyors are always available. We can work with you to design and build a larger system.

Finishing

Screeds After **placing** concrete, don't forget to **finish** it! These large bars **strike off** a concrete surface, removing the excess and leaving an even surface behind.

Floats and trowels: For the final touches, we have a variety of floats and trowels available. They come in various shapes and sizes. They are either hand tools or motorized.

Get ready!

❶ Before you read the passage, talk about these questions.

1 What is one machine that mixes cement?

2 What can be used to transport small loads around a site?

Reading

❷ Read the website for a construction supply company. Then, choose the correct answers.

1 Why is a countercurrent mixer especially useful?

   A It has a discharge chute.

   B It produces more agitation.

   C It has a capacity of 170 liters.

   D It can be moved with a crane.

2 Which of the following is NOT readily available in multiple sizes?

   A buggies   C wheelbarrows

   B buckets   D belt conveyors

3 What is the purpose of a strike-off bar?

   A to remove excess concrete

   B to mix additives and colors

   C to move concrete around a worksite

   D to put the finishing touches on concrete

Vocabulary

❸ Match the words (1-7) with the definitions (A-G).

1 __ finish   5 __ belt conveyor

2 __ mixing   6 __ uniformity

3 __ float   7 __ place

4 __ buggy

A to put concrete in its final position

B a small man-powered or motorized vehicle used to transport materials at a construction site

C the process of combining and stirring cement, water, and aggregate until it forms a concrete mix

D a rectangular tool used to smooth and level the top layer of concrete

E the state of being the same or alike throughout

F to alter concrete surfaces to produce the desired final appearance and texture

G a machine for transporting concrete or other material that consists of two pulleys and a continuous loop of material that rotates around them

4 Fill in the blanks with the correct words and phrases from the word bank.

drum mixer   trowel   chute
wheelbarrow
strike off   bucket
countercurrent mixer

1 The concrete will travel down the _____ with only gravity needed to move it.

2 The blades inside this _____ do not move.

3 Use a _____ _____ to make sure the surface is smooth.

4 A crane will lift this _____ to move the concrete to the top level.

5 The blades in a _____ rotate in a different direction than the pan.

6 Push this _____ over there and dump out the concrete.

7 A screed is used to _____ the finished concrete.

5 🎧 Listen and read the website for a construction supply company again. What tools are available for finishing concrete?

Listening

6 🎧 Listen to a conversation between a contractor and an employee. Mark the following statements as true (T) or false (F).

1 __ The concrete should not fall more than a meter when being placed.

2 __ The concrete should be placed in one spot and moved around the final surface.

3 __ Trowels and floats can be used right after the concrete is struck off.

7 🎧 Listen again and complete the conversation.

Contractor:	Yes. You can use a **1** _____ to place it. But don't dump it off this edge. It can't fall more than a meter.
Employee:	Why's that?
Contractor:	If it falls too far, the water might **2** _____ _____ the other ingredients.
Employee:	I see. I'll definitely **3** _____ _____ then.
Contractor:	Also, make sure you place the concrete as close to its **4** _____ _____ as possible. That's better than spreading it around.
Employee:	That **5** _____ _____ . Shouldn't be too hard.
Contractor:	Good. After you place it, use a screed to **6** _____ _____ _____ and smooth out the surface.
Employee:	Right. And then I use floats and trowels to even out the small rough areas?
Contractor:	Yes. But you have to wait a while for the surface to become more solid first.
Employee:	Okay, I can do that.
Contractor:	Just don't wait too long, or we'll be stuck with an uneven surface.

Speaking

8 With a partner, act out the roles below based on Task 7. Then, switch roles.

USE LANGUAGE SUCH AS:

Make sure you ... / After you place it ...
You have to ...

Student A: You are a contractor. Talk to Student B about:
• instructions for placing and finishing concrete
• why to be careful when placing the concrete
• why to be careful when finishing the concrete

Student B: You are an employee. Talk to Student A about instructions for placing and finishing concrete.

Writing

9 Use the website and the conversation from Task 8 to write instructions for placing and finishing concrete. Write about:

• placing   • finishing   • final touches

Introduction to Timber frames

glued-laminated timber

glulam rivet

Split-ring connector

pin type connection

truss plates

shear plates

Timber is lightweight, strong, and inexpensive. That's why it has been used in structural frames for centuries. Such frames must be able to support heavy loads. This includes the **dead load**, or the weight of the building itself. Also included are moving **live loads**, such as weather elements. Timber frames are allowed to move to a certain extent under such loads. The amount of movement allowed is known as a **deflection** limit.

Timber frames **transfer** loads to capable load-bearing structures and the foundation with **timber connectors**. The types of connectors used will depend on the building's materials and structural requirements. Timber frame connectors often have **pin-type connections**. They connect pieces through plates and bolts, and allow for some rotation between pieces. Specific types of connectors include:

Glulam rivets – These are special steel nails used to connect pieces of **glued-laminated timber**.

Shear plates – These plates are designed to prevent timber deformation by spreading pressure over a large area of wood. They can be used for wood-to-wood or steel-to-wood connections.

Split-ring connectors – These are similar to shear plates but transfer a load through a ring instead of a bolt. They can only be used for wood-to-wood connections.

Truss plates – These special plates connect timber of the same thickness in the same plane.

Get ready!

1 **Before you read the passage, talk about these questions.**

1 What type of building might have a timber frame?

2 What are some different types of timber connectors?

Reading

2 **Read the construction manual on timber frames. Then, mark the following statements as true (T) or false (F).**

1 __ It is normal for wind or snow to move a wooden frame slightly.

2 __ Pin-type connections prevent rotation between pieces of timber.

3 __ Split-ring connectors are only for wood-to-wood connections.

Vocabulary

3 **Match the words (1-6) with the definitions (A-F).**

1 __ truss plate   4 __ shear plate

2 __ glulam rivet   5 __ pin-type connection

3 __ deflection   6 __ transfer

A a special steel nail used in connections of glued-laminated timber

B a device that distributes force over a large area of timber in order to prevent damage

C a timber connector that uses thin plates and bolts to join timber pieces, which allows for some rotation between the pieces

D a metal plate used to connect timber of the same thickness in the same plane

E to move the pressure of a load from one structure or object to another

F a measure of how much a piece of timber changes shape under the pressure of a load

4 **Read the sentence pairs. Choose which word or phrase best fits each blank.**

1 live loads / dead loads

   A Structural designs must consider _____ such as wind or movable objects.

   B _____ include the weight of the building itself.

2 glued-laminated timber / timber connector

   A What kind of _____ is joining these two pieces?

   B Strong adhesive is used to hold this _____ together.

3 split-ring connector / timber

   A A _____ does not use bolts to move the weight of the load.

   B _____ cannot support as much weight as concrete.

5 🎧 **Listen and read the construction manual on timber frames again. What connections can shear plates be used for?**

Listening

6 🎧 **Listen to a conversation between a new construction worker and a manager. Choose the correct answers.**

1 What is the conversation mainly about?

   A why ring-type connections are stronger than bolt-type connections

   B where steel-to-wood connections are required

   C reasons to use glued-laminated timber

   D where to use different types of timber connectors

2 What should the man use for steel-to-wood connections?

   A split-ring connectors   C shear plates

   B glulam rivets   D truss plates

Timber frames

7 🎧 **Listen again and complete the conversation.**

Manager:	That can be difficult to **1** _____ _____ _____ . What do you have a question about?
Worker:	Well, I know that **2** _____ _____ are specially made to connect glued-laminated timber.
Manager:	Yes, that one's pretty easy. The name tells you **3** _____ _____ _____ .
Worker:	Right. What about split-ring connectors then? Can I use those to connect a timber frame to **4** _____ _____ ?
Manager:	No. Those connectors are for **5** _____ - _____ - _____ connections only.
Worker:	I see. What should I use there instead?
Manager:	Use **6** _____ _____ . They're good for distributing a load over a large area.

Speaking

8 **With a partner, act out the roles below based on Task 7. Then, switch roles.**

USE LANGUAGE SUCH AS:

Can I use those ...?

Those are for ...

They're not designed for ...

Student A: You are a construction worker. Talk to Student B about:

• different types of timber connectors

• where to use different connectors

• the strengths of different connectors

Student B: You are a manager. Talk to Student A about different types of timber connectors.

Writing

9 **Use the manual and the conversation from Task 8 to write the construction worker's notes on timber frame connectors. Write about:**

• some different types of connectors

bearing plates

anchor bolt

Steel frame CONSTRUCTION

Safety Guidelines

There are several important safety concerns when constructing a **steel frame**. First, ensure that each **member** is in the correct position. Do so by locating the **erection mark** on each piece. This will tell you how the **section shape** fits together.

Next, if using a **bolting** connection, use the correct size and strength of bolt. Bolts are labeled by their **ASTM designation**. An A307 bolt is not suitable for a job requiring an A325, and vice versa. Also be sure to use the proper type of connection. A **bearing-type connection** should be used where the applied load mainly pulls in one direction. **Friction-type connections** can be used where the load direction varies. When drilling holes, pay attention to the standard **pitch** and **gauge** distances for that structural shape.

Welding also has particular connections for specific jobs. Use **fillet welds** as much as possible. They do not require preparation of the welded material. However, a **groove weld** is safer if a very strong connection is needed.

When erecting a steel frame, place **anchor bolts** carefully. This allows the **bearing plates** to be positioned accurately. These plates will hold the **columns** of the frame in place, with **girders** connecting between the columns. Last, **open-web steel joists** or bar joists are often used to support roofs and floors.

Get ready!

1 Before you read the passage, talk about these questions.

1 What type of frame is used for high-rise buildings?

2 What is one type of bolt used to connect steel frames?

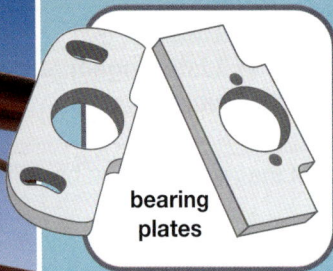

Reading

2 Read the safety guidelines for steel frame construction. Then, choose the correct answers.

1 What does an erection mark do?
   A indicates what kind of connection to use
   B shows how a section shape fits together
   C shows the strength and size of a bolt
   D indicates a pitch and gauge distance

2 When should a bearing-type connection be used?
   A when no preparation of the material is needed
   B where the load direction varies
   C when a very strong connection is needed
   D where the load mainly pulls in one direction

3 Which of the following frame components is placed first?
   A girders   C anchor bolts
   B bearing plates   D columns

Vocabulary

3 Match the words (1-9) with the definitions (A-I).

1 __ girder   6 __ column
2 __ groove weld   7 __ gauge
3 __ bolting   8 __ fillet weld
4 __ pitch   9 __ member
5 __ open-web steel joist

A the distance between a row of bolts in a steel frame connection

B a type of welding used in steel frame construction that joins pieces of metal that are at 90 degree angles

C an individual piece of a structural frame, made of steel, timber, or concrete

D the primary horizontal piece of a steel frame

E a type of welding used in steel frame construction that does not require preparation on the material that is welded

F a lightweight truss used to support a roof or floor in steel frame construction

G the distance between the center of holes in a row of bolts in a steel frame connection

H the primary vertical piece of a steel frame

I the use of strong cylindrical metal fasteners to join pieces of a steel frame

4 Fill in the blanks with the correct words and phrases:
ASTM designation, *erection mark*, *anchor bolt*, *friction-type connection*, *section shape*, *bearing plate*, *bearing-type connection*, *steel frame*.

1 The wide flange is a common steel frame _____ .

2 Use a strong _____ to secure the frame to the foundation.

3 That bolt has a(n) _____ of A325.

4 A building with a(n) _____ can be built many stories high.

5 The bolt transfers the load in a(n) _____ .

6 Look at the _____ to tell where this piece goes.

7 Anchor bolts are fastened into a(n) _____ .

8 A load is transfered along connected pieces in a _____ .

5 🎧 **Listen and read the safety guidelines for steel frame construction again. What are some safety guidelines in steel frame construction?**

Listening

6 🎧 **Listen to a conversation between two construction workers. Mark the following statements as true (T) or false (F).**

1 ___ The workers debate which type of weld to use.

2 ___ The workers will use a friction-type connection.

3 ___ The woman suggested using the wrong gauge distance.

7 🎧 **Listen again and complete the conversation.**

Worker 1:	Okay. What **1** _____ _____ _____ do we need?
Worker 2:	Hmm. I **2** _____ _____ _____ some A307s.
Worker 1:	Are you sure? **3** _____ _____ _____ were only for temporary connections.
Worker 2:	Let me check. Oh yeah, you're right. We **4** _____ _____ _____ A325s. Sorry, I was confused for a minute.
Worker 1:	No problem. Do we need to use a **5** _____ - _____ _____ ?
Worker 2:	I don't think so. The **6** _____ _____ varies here and it shouldn't hurt the connection.
Worker 1:	So we can use a friction-type connection. In that case, we'll have to be sure to tighten the bolts properly to give good tension.
Worker 2:	Right. Okay, I think we're ready to get started.
Worker 1:	Wait. Do you know the standard pitch and gauge distances for this shape?

Speaking

8 With a partner, act out the roles below based on Task 7. Then, switch roles.

USE LANGUAGE SUCH AS:

What size ...?

I think we need ...

Do you know ...?

Student A: You are a construction worker. Talk to Student B about:

• a steel frame connection

• what kind of connection to use

• checking the details of the connection

Student B: You are a construction worker. Talk to Student A about a steel frame connection.

Writing

9 Use the safety guidelines and the conversation from Task 8 to write the worker's instructions for connecting parts of a steel frame. Write about:

• bolting or welding

• the type of connection

• gauge information

8 | Concrete Frames

lap splice

concrete frame

welded splice

mechanical splice

couplers

welded wire reinforcement

RZY STEEL — Reinforcing Steel in Concrete Frames

Just because your structure has a **concrete frame** does not mean you won't need steel components. Plain concrete is **brittle** and subject to serious failure. Steel **reinforcement** is an essential part of a concrete frame to improve its **tensile strength**. RZY Steel provides the reinforcing bars necessary to guarantee a long, secure life for your structure. They can be applied to either a **precast** concrete frame or one that is cast-in-place, as well as to **prestressed** concrete.

When evaluating your reinforcing steel needs, you should keep a few considerations in mind. First, there must be enough **cover** to protect the steel from the environment. Second, our steel bars come in certain sizes. You will likely need to **splice** them together on site. It is important to know the proper kind of splice for your job. A **lap splice** is very common and easy. A **mechanical splice** may be used when bars have large diameters. We can supply you with the **couplers** required for this splice. We also manufacture special steel that is well-suited to a **welded splice**.

In addition to bars, we also make **wire mesh** used in **welded wire reinforcement**. This type of reinforcement is easy to place with large concrete slabs.

Get ready!

1 Before you read the passage, talk about these questions.

1 What type of reinforcement uses wire mesh?

2 What are some different ways to splice reinforcing steel?

Reading

2 Read the website from a rebar and coupler manufacturer. Then, mark the following statements as true (T) or false (F).

1 __ Reinforcing steel is not needed with cast-in-place concrete frames.

2 __ A coupler is needed for a mechanical splice.

3 __ Wire mesh works well with concrete slabs.

Vocabulary

3 Match the words (1-8) with the definitions (A-H).

1 __ wire mesh   4 __ splice   7 __ cover
2 __ reinforcement 5 __ precast   8 __ prestressed
3 __ coupler   6 __ brittle

A something that is placed over something else in order to hide or protect it

B formed and cured at a plant and brought to a building site

C breaks or snaps easily

D a device used to splice pieces of reinforced steel consisting of two female ends

E to permanently join pieces of reinforcing steel together

F concrete that has had tendons added to overcome its weakness in tension

G something that is added to something else to make it stronger

H a material made of wire rods formed into grids with little spacing between wires, used to reinforce concrete

4 **Read the sentence pairs. Choose which word or phrase best fits each blank.**

1 concrete frame / lap splice

  A A _____ is the most common way to join reinforcing steel together.

  B This _____ needs to be reinforced with steel to be stronger.

2 welded splice / welded wire reinforcement

  A Special reinforcing steel is used because a _____ needs a lot of heat.

  B This concrete is reinforced by a sheet of _____ .

3 tensile strength / mechanical splice

  A Reinforcement is required to overcome concrete's lack of _____ .

  B A metal sleeve joins pieces of steel in a _____ .

5 🎧 **Listen and read the website for a rebar and coupler manufacturer again. What products does the company sell?**

Listening

6 🎧 **Listen to a conversation between a contractor and a worker. Choose the correct answers.**

1 What is the conversation mainly about?

  A the benefits of a concrete frame

  B why welded splices are necessary

  C requirements for a new framing job

  D why rebars are better than wire mesh reinforcement

2 Why does the client not like lap splices?

  A They do not look good.

  B They are too expensive.

  C They are not strong enough.

  D They take too long to install.

RZY RZY Steel
RZY STEEL for Concrete Frames

7 🎧 **Listen sten again and complete the conversation.**

Contractor:	The pieces we ordered are all **1** _____ _____ segments.
Worker:	So we'll need to do a lot of splicing.
Contractor:	Right. We have a few different **2** _____ _____ available.
Worker:	Well, there's always lap splicing. That's the quickest and **3** _____ _____ way to do it, right?
Contractor:	Yes, but the client doesn't like **4** _____ _____ . They think it's not secure enough.
Worker:	That's too bad. **5** _____ _____ _____ _____ instead?
Contractor:	Well, the client paid for larger diameter bars. They're **6** _____ _____ mechanical splices.

Speaking

8 **With a partner, act out the roles below based on Task 7. Then, switch roles.**

> **USE LANGUAGE SUCH AS:**
>
> *Our next project will be ...*
> *We'll use ...*
> *That client doesn't like ...*

Student A: You are a contractor on a new concrete frame project. Talk to Student B about:
- what kind of reinforcement to use
- the client's opinion of a kind of splicing

Student B: You are a worker. Talk to Student A about a new concrete frame project.

Writing

9 **Use the website and the conversation from Task 8 to write a project summary. Write about:**

- the kind of project
- the need for reinforcement
- the kind of splicing that will be used

casement

frame sashes

revolving doors

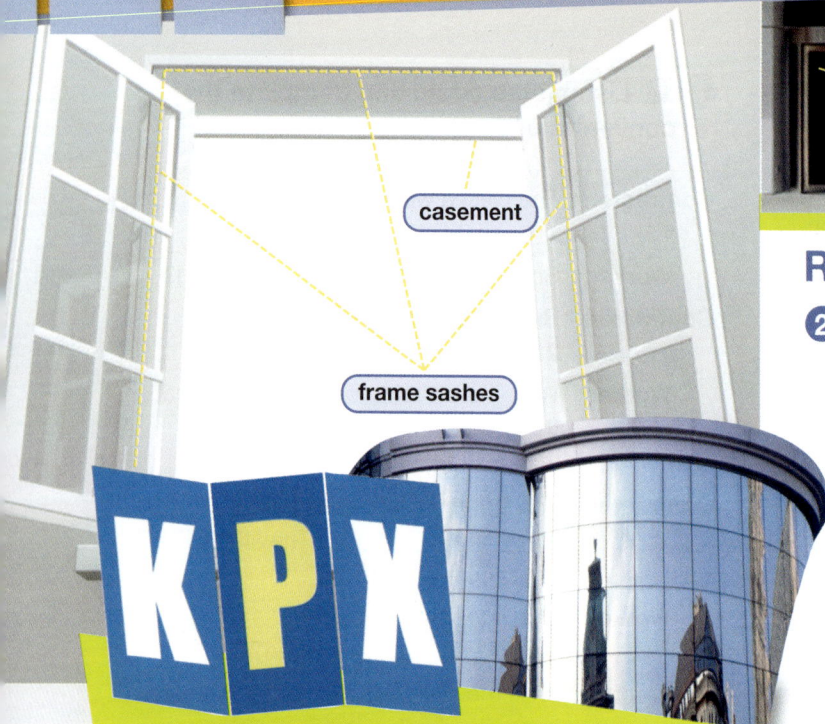

KPX Doors and Windows
Product Lineup

KPX Doors and Windows offers a wide selection of products to fit your building needs. We make **fixed** and opening windows for every type of building. Sash windows may be either single or **double-hung**. Note that the placement of hinges determines the type of sash window and how it opens. A **casement** window has hinges on its side, a **hopper** window has hinges on the bottom, and an **awning** window has hinges on top. All are manufactured by KPX. Horizontally **sliding** windows are available in single panes. We can also cut **frame sashes** to your custom dimensions and number of **panes**.

Every building needs doors, and KPX supplies them for every look and purpose. Exterior and interior **fire doors** of various ratings are available to protect your building's occupants. **Revolving doors** are an excellent method of permitting lots of traffic while preventing heat loss or gain from drafts. **Automatic doors** triggered by pressure or motion sensors are ideal for large stores. If space is limited, a **pocket door** eliminates the need to have clearance for a swinging door. Last, **bifold doors** are perfect for interior openings such as closets.

Please contact customer service at service@kpx.com for more information about the KPX line of products.

Get ready!

① **Before you read the passage, talk about these questions.**

1 What are some types of doors that might be used in a hospital?

2 What is one type of window?

Reading

② **Read the product descriptions from a door and window supplier. Then, choose the correct answers.**

1 What is true of the company's windows?

   A Fixed windows are no longer available.

   B Sliding windows have multiple panes.

   C Sash windows may only be single hung.

   D Frame sashes are available in custom sizes.

2 What kind of window has hinges on the bottom?

   A an awning window   **C** a hopper window

   B a casement window   **D** a fixed window

3 What is a benefit of revolving doors?

   A They save space.

   B They are ideal for large stores.

   C They protect a building's occupants.

   D They preserve a building's internal temperature.

Vocabulary

③ **Match the words (1-7) with the definitions (A-G).**

1 __ sliding door   5 __ double-hung

2 __ bifold door   6 __ revolving door

3 __ fixed   7 __ pane

4 __ automatic door

A a door with several sections that fold into pairs, often used as a closet door

B a window with two parts that overlap slightly and slide up and down inside its frame

C a door with three or four separate doors that attach to a central shaft and rotate within an enclosed space

D a window or door that opens by moving horizontally

E a door powered by electricity that opens on its own upon detection of motion or pressure

F unable to be opened

G a section of glass in a window

4 Read the sentence pairs. Choose which word or phrase best fits each blank.

1 casement / awning

   A A(n) _____ window swings outward, with hinges at its top.

   B This _____ window has two hinges on each side.

2 hopper / frame sash

   A This _____ holds six panes of glass.

   B A _____ window has hinges at its bottom.

3 pocket door / fire door

   A A _____ saves space by sliding into the wall.

   B This _____ will prevent the spread of smoke through the building.

5 🎧 Listen and read the product descriptions from a door and window supplier again. What are some of the products the company offers?

Listening

6 🎧 Listen to a conversation between an architect and a building owner. Mark the statements true (T) or false (F).

1 __ The man is drawing building plans for the woman.

2 __ The woman has casement windows on her house.

3 __ The woman chooses sash windows for the building.

7 🎧 Listen again and complete the conversation.

Owner:	Hi, Marty. This is Rachel Swanson. Your office is drawing up the plans for my new building.
Architect:	Ah, yes. How can I help you, Ms. Swanson?
Owner:	I wanted to talk about the **1** _____ _____ _____ to install.
Architect:	Sure. Do you **2** _____ _____ _____ of what you want?
Owner:	Not really. I'm afraid I **3** _____ _____ _____ about different window types.
Architect:	Well, **4** _____ _____ are very common in this area. They have one or two **5** _____ _____ that slide up and down.
Owner:	Of course! I have those in my house.
Architect:	Before you decide, **6** _____ _____ _____ that you could also go with casement windows.
Owner:	What are those, exactly?
Architect:	They have sashes that swing in or out, like a door.

Speaking

8 With a partner, act out the roles below based on Task 7. Then, switch roles.

Student A: You are an architect. Talk to Student B about:

• installing doors or windows in a new building

• different options

• something the owner should know

Student B: You are a building owner. Talk to Student A about installing doors or windows in a new building.

Writing

9 Use the product descriptions and the conversation from Task 8 to write an email from an architect to a building owner. Write about:

• several door or window choices

• how each works

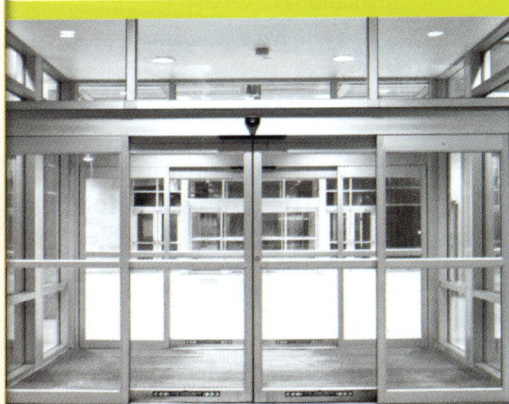

automatic door

10 Insulation

JOS Contractors

Insulation Work Order

Type(s) of Insulation

_____	spray polyurethane foam
_____	glass wool blanket
_____	insulating concrete form
__X__	natural fiber
__X__	rigid panel
__X__	loose fill

Structure: This insulation order is for a two-floor wood frame house. It has a crawl space and an attic.

┌─ Order Summary ──────────────

This project involves the complete replacement of insulation in an older house. First, any **asbestos** insulation that is found must be carefully removed. Then we can begin to install the new insulation. The owner would like to use natural fiber insulation. We have ordered rigid panels made of wool and bound with polyester for this job. Wool has the highest **R-value** of any natural fiber. It is also an effective **vapor retarder**, so it is appropriate for the exterior walls. It has been treated with fire and insect retardants. There should be sufficient **batts** on site already to cover the entire **building envelope**. Should there be a shortage, contact the office and we'll deliver more.

The batts of wool panels will not fit into small spaces, especially in the attic and crawl space. For these areas, there is a supply of loose fill made from granulated cork at the job site.

Get ready!

1 Before you read the passage, talk about these questions.

1 What is one natural material that can be used for insulation?

2 What is the name for a section of panel insulation?

Reading

2 Read the work order for insulation installation. Then, mark the following statements as true (T) or false (F).

1 __ Polyester has the highest R-value of any natural fiber.

2 __ The wool panels have already been delivered to the house.

3 __ The company will use insulating concrete foam where batts will not fit.

spray polyurethane foam

natural fiber

batt

Vocabulary

3 Match the words (1-6) with the definitions (A-F).

1 __ vapor retarder   4 __ loose fill

2 __ building envelope   5 __ rigid panel

3 __ glass wool blanket   6 __ R-value

A a kind of building insulation made from fibrous materials or plastic foam, often sold in sections

B a rating of an insulation material's effectiveness

C a type of insulation that does not have a solid form and therefore can be blown or sprayed into small spaces

D a piece of fiberglass insulation that is sold in a continuous roll

E a material that resists penetration by moisture, placed in building walls, floors, and ceilings

F the part of the building that separates the inside from the outside, including walls, doors, and windows

4 Fill in the blanks with the correct words and phrases from the word bank.

WORD BANK

spray polyurethane foam   batt   natural fiber insulation   asbestos   insulating concrete form

1 This house uses cotton as a(n) _____ insulator.

2 We put in a(n) _____ that remained after construction to serve as insulation.

3 Any _____ that you find in this old house will have to be removed.

4 A(n) _____ of rigid panel insulation will fit well in this wall cavity.

5 What kind of _____ will you use to keep heat inside the building?

6 _____ expands to fill all the spaces in a wall.

22

5 🎧 Listen and read the work order for insulation installation again. What kind of insulation is being installed?

Listening

6 🎧 Listen to a conversation between a contractor and subcontractor. Choose the correct answers.

1 What is the conversation mainly about?

   A whether a client can afford to add loose fill

   B why to use rigid panels instead of polyurethane foam

   C why the subcontractor installed rigid panels

   D where to install certain kinds of installation

2 Why is the man concerned about using rigid panels inside?

   A They are very expensive.

   B They will not fill small areas.

   C They are not very effective.

   D They take a long time to install.

7 🎧 Listen again and complete the conversation.

Contractor:	He wants to use spray polyurethane foam in the 1 _____ _____ .
Subcontractor:	That should be fine. It'll block off the 2 _____ _____ by expanding into all the little gaps.
Contractor:	That's what I thought. Then, he'd like to use 3 _____ _____ of polystyrene foam in the interior walls.
Subcontractor:	Hmm. I'm 4 _____ _____ _____ about that. It'll be fine in some places, but it won't fit in every space.
Contractor:	5 _____ _____ . What should we do about that?
Subcontractor:	Well. like I said, we can use the rigid panels for the big wall spaces. But I would also recommend getting some 6 _____ _____ for the small areas.

Speaking

8 With a partner, act out the roles below based on Task 7. Then, switch roles.

Student A: You are a contractor. Talk to Student B about:

• the kinds of insulation for a project

• where each insulation will be installed

• Student B's concern about the project

Student B: You are a subcontractor. Talk to Student A about the kinds of insulation for a project.

Writing

9 Use the work order and the conversation from Task 8 to write the subcontractor's notes. Write about:

• insulation for the exterior walls and interior walls

• concerns about small spaces

11 Stairs

When constructing a **flight** of **stairs**, the first step is to install the **stringer** that will support the staircase. Different kinds of stringers can be used for stairs made of wood, steel, or concrete. Next, determine the correct number of **risers** and **treads**. Divide the vertical distance from one floor to the next by the desired **riser height**. The result will be the number of risers needed. The number of treads is determined by dividing the horizontal distance by the desired **tread depth**. A **nosing** can extend each tread to provide for a secure foothold. The **going** of each step should be easily covered in a single step. Also, remember that **landings** must be placed to divide a long staircase into smaller sections.

A handrail is an important safety feature of every staircase. You may need to install a special **balustrade** to a decorative set of stairs. First, install a **newel** at each end to support the balustrade. Then, install the **baluster** columns and place the **banister** rail on top. Last, if there is a floor beneath it, the **spandrel** underneath the staircase can be used for storage or some other function. Otherwise, it can be closed off.

Installing Stairs: Instructions and Measurements

riser
nosing
tread
balustrade
baluster
newel

Get ready!

1 Before you read the passage, talk about these questions.

1 What are some parts of a staircase?
2 What does a person hold when walking down stairs?

Reading

2 Read the instructions on installing stairs. Then, choose the correct answers.

1 What is the first step to constructing a flight of stairs?
  A install the stringer
  B install the balustrade
  C ensure the tread is safe
  D divide the vertical distance by the riser height

2 How can tread depth be increased?
  A add a nosing   C install larger newels
  B reduce the going   D insert landings

3 Which of the following is NOT part of a balustrade?
  A baluster   C newel
  B spandrel   D banister

Vocabulary

3 Match the words (1-8) with the definitions (A-H).

1 __ stringer   5 __ baluster
2 __ going   6 __ landing
3 __ tread   7 __ banister
4 __ stairs   8 __ riser

A a short column used as part of a group to support a rail on the side of a staircase
B the vertical part of a step
C the distance from the edge of a nosing to the edge of nosing in plan view
D steps that connect two floors in a building
E the handrail of a staircase.
F the structural part of a staircase that supports the risers and treads
G a platform at the bottom, at the top, or in between sets of stairs
H the horizontal part of a step

4 Read the sentences and choose the correct words or phrases.

1 The building has ten **flights / nosings** of stairs.

2 Measure the **riser height / spandrel** underneath this set of stairs.

3 Each step should have a **spandrel / tread depth** of 30 cm to be safe.

4 Each tread on this staircase has a 3 cm **nosing / newel**.

5 This is a lovely **balustrade / flight** with wooden columns.

6 This staircase is supported by a strong **baluster / newel** at each end.

7 Code requires that each step cannot have a **riser height / stringer** more than 18 cm.

5 🎧 Listen and read the instructions on installing stairs again. What can stairs be made of?

Listening

6 🎧 Listen to a conversation between a contractor and employee. Mark the following statements as true (T) or false (F).

1 __ The woman drilled too deep into the newel.

2 __ The crew is currently building the landing.

3 __ The project will be behind schedule.

7 🎧 Listen again and complete the conversation.

Employee:	I'm **1** _____ _____ _____ problem, Sir.
Contractor:	Yeah, I heard that there was a delay. **2** _____ _____ , exactly?
Employee:	Well, I **3** _____ _____ _____ into the newel to support the balusters. We had to take that one out and install a new one.
Contractor:	How long **4** _____ _____ _____ ?
Employee:	It set me back a couple of hours. **5** _____ _____ _____ about all this, Sir.
Contractor:	It's all right. Just please try to be more careful in the future. We're on a very **6** _____ _____ .
Employee:	I understand, Sir. I'll try my best to be both quick and accurate.
Contractor:	Good. So what are you doing now?
Employee:	We're installing the **7** _____ _____ now.
Contractor:	Good. Will you have the banister installed by the end of the day?
Employee:	Absolutely.

Speaking

8 With a partner, act out the roles below based on Task 7. Then, switch roles.

Student A: You are a contractor. Talk to Student B about:

• a delay in building a staircase

• what the crew is working on now

• when the staircase will be done

Student B: You are an employee. Talk to Student A about a delay in building a staircase.

Writing

9 Use the instructions and the conversation from Task 8 to write a progress report on the construction of stairs. Write about:

• the completed steps

• a delay

• when the remaining steps will be complete

25

SUE GABLE

Expert Mason

mortar

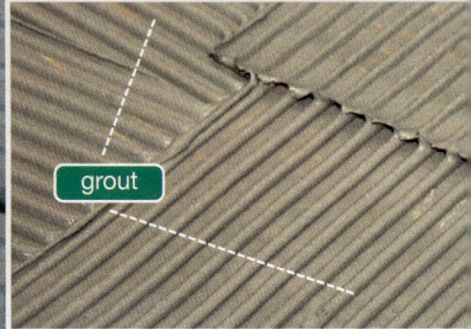

grout

curtain wall

Whether you want a decorative brick wall or a complete brick building, I am the **mason** for you. I have over 20 years of **masonry** experience. My recent work includes:

- leading the installation of the exterior **bearing wall** at the Two Oaks Shopping Center

- designing and installing numerous **curtain walls** in the Fair Meadows housing project

- installing a complex **multiwythe cavity wall** at the Jefferson Government Building

With my experience, I can recommend the right design for your needs. For example, do you need room for drainage but still want a brick wall? A **single wythe veneer** wall with airspace backing is right for you.

I've used every type of **masonry unit**, including brick, concrete, and limestone. I can make the perfect **mortar** mix for any material to guarantee a strong, long-lived wall. I am also familiar with using **grout** to embed steel reinforcement in a wall.

I would be happy to visit your building site for a free consultation. Please call me at (797) 555-2356 or email sue@gablemasonry.com.

Get ready!

1 **Before you read the passage, talk about these questions.**

1 What material does a mason work with?
2 What connects bricks in a brick wall?

Reading

2 **Read the ad for a mason. Then, mark the following statements as true (T) or false (F).**

1 __ The mason recently completed a single wythe veneer wall.

2 __ The mason mixes her own mortar.

3 __ Grout is used to embed brick into a wall.

Vocabulary

3 **Match the words (1-6) with the definitions (A-F).**

1 __ cavity wall   4 __ veneer
2 __ single wythe   5 __ curtain wall
3 __ bearing wall   6 __ multiwythe

A a wall with a thickness of one block

B a wall that bears a weight down to a foundation structure

C a wall with a thickness of two or more blocks

D a wall that has one masonry layer backed by an airspace

E a wall that is non-structural and only serves to keep out the weather

F a wall that has two skins made from brick or concrete separated by a hollow space

4 **Fill in the blanks with the correct words and phrases from the word bank.**

WORD BANK

masonry unit   mortar
masonry   mason   grout

1 Use a special _____ to embed the rebar in this wall.

2 The construction company is hiring a new _____ .

3 Use standard _____ to join the bricks together.

4 This concrete _____ weighs eight kilograms.

5 _____ involves the use of many materials other than bricks and cement.

5 🎧 **Listen and read the ad for a mason again. What types of walls has the mason recently created?**

Listening

6 🎧 **Listen to a conversation between a mason and a potential customer. Choose the correct answers.**

1   What is the conversation mainly about?
   A   the benefits of masonry
   B   when construction can begin
   C   how masonry can lower construction costs
   D   why masonry is being used more often

2   Why does the woman recommend using masonry?
   A   It is less expensive.
   B   It looks more attractive.
   C   It lasts longer than other materials.
   D   It can be constructed faster than other materials.

7 🎧 **Listen again and complete the conversation.**

Customer:	Hi, Sue. My name is Dave Chandler. I'm considering a new office for my business. I'm thinking of going with masonry.
Mason:	That's a great idea. What can I tell you?
Customer:	Well, I don't know too much about it. Is it really **1** _____ _____ _____ than a timber or concrete frame?
Mason:	I think so. Masonry has a lot of benefits.
Customer:	How so?
Mason:	For one, masonry structures **2** _____ _____ _____ _____ than other kinds of structures.
Customer:	Oh, yeah? How much longer?
Mason:	A well-built brick structure has a life of more than fifty years. That's **3** _____ _____ thirty years for steel or reinforced concrete.
Customer:	That's impressive. But **4** _____ _____ _____ , I won't need this building in fifty years.
Mason:	**5** _____ _____ . But it will increase the value of your property. That could be important if you decide to sell it.
Customer:	I guess that **6** _____ _____ .

Speaking

8 **With a partner, act out the roles below based on Task 7. Then, switch roles.**

USE LANGUAGE SUCH AS:

I'm considering ...
For one, masonry structures ...
To be honest, ...

Student A: You are a mason. Talk to Student B about:
- masonry and other frame types
- the strength of masonry
- the value of masonry

Student B: You are considering masonry for a new building. Talk to Student A about masonry.

Writing

9 **Use the ad and the conversation from Task 8 to write an informational brochure about masonry walls. Write about:**
- types of masonry walls
- materials used
- benefits of masonry

mason

roof frame

parapet

scupper gutter

Roofing Guide: Preventing Water Damage

Water that enters a building through the **roof** can cause significant damage. The **roof frame**, the **roof deck**, insulation, and personal property can all be damaged. Serving as an effective **vapor barrier** is thus a roof's most important job.

Leaks often occur near **flashings** that penetrate the **roof membrane**. Inspect the seals at the locations frequently. **Rain** that flows over a **drain's** seal can also lead to problems. Drains should be wide enough to handle a heavy rainfall and should be cleaned often. An increased **slope** around the drain can help avoid pooling of water in the area.

Roof leaks also typically occur at roof edges, such as along **parapet** walls and **walks**. Custom-made components can be installed to seal a roof perimeter. **Scuppers** in parapets and **gutters** along edges should be cleaned regularly. Otherwise, water is unable to flow away from the roof. A properly installed **gravel stop** can prevent gravel from clogging gutters and other drains.

A roof must protect a building against the full variety of **elements** experienced in its climate. For example, roofs in cold climates need to withstand the weight of **snow** and be sloped sufficiently to reduce accumulation.

Get ready!

1 **Before you read the passage, talk about these questions.**

1 What carries rainwater off a roof?
2 What is the main structural support of a roof called?

Reading

2 **Read the troubleshooting article on roofs. Then, choose the correct answers.**

1 According to the passage, what is the most important job of a roof?
   A preventing heat loss
   B stopping moisture leaks
   C supporting the building frame
   D withstanding the weight of elements

2 Which of the following is NOT listed as a place where roof leaks occur?
   A a roof deck   C a drain's seal
   B a parapet wall   D a flashing

3 How can a roof perimeter be protected from water leaks?
   A increasing the roof slope
   B increasing the width of drains
   C inspecting flashing seals
   D installing custom components

Vocabulary

3 **Match the words (1-8) with the definitions (A-H).**

1 __ gutter   5 __ vapor barrier
2 __ parapet   6 __ roof membrane
3 __ roof deck   7 __ scupper
4 __ flashing   8 __ gravel stop

A an opening in a wall that allows water to drain off of a roof

B a layer of roofing material in between the structural parts and insulating or waterproofing layers

C a roof component used to seal roof edges where the roof covering is interrupted

D a piece of metal placed at the edge of a roof to prevent gravel from falling off

E a part of a building's edge, such as a wall, that extends above the roof

F a layer of rubber or bitumen placed typically over a flat roof to prevent water leakage

G a channel at the edge of a roof that collects rainwater and carries it away

H a material that prevents moisture from entering a wall, roof, or floor

4 Read the sentence pairs. Choose which word or phrase best fits each blank.

1 snow / rain

   A _____ builds up on roofs in the winter because it does not flow like water.

   B _____ should be directed off a roof into gutters as it falls.

2 slope / elements

   A A roof membrane protects a flat roof against the _____ .

   B Even a flat roof has a small _____ so rain flows away.

3 walk / drain

   A The old house had a long _____ along its roof.

   B Water is collecting on this roof without a proper _____ .

4 roof / roof frame

   A Parts of a _____ could be made of timber, steel, or concrete.

   B In some areas, a flat _____ is very popular.

5 🎧 Listen and read the troubleshooting article on roofs again. How can leaks at a roof drain be prevented?

Listening

6 🎧 Listen to a conversation between a contractor and a homeowner. Mark the following statements as true (T) or false (F).

1 __ There were several leaks around the edge of the roof.

2 __ Leaves and mud were clogging the gutters.

3 __ The woman will return regularly to clean the gutters.

7 🎧 Listen again and complete the conversation.

Homeowner:	I see. Anything else?
Contractor:	Yes, I noticed there was some gravel collecting **1** _____ _____ _____ . That can block rain from draining off and add to the leak problem.
Homeowner:	**2** _____ _____ _____ . How did you fix that?
Contractor:	I installed a few **3** _____ _____ that will keep it from happening. Then I cleaned out the gutters, so they'll work fine.
Homeowner:	I see. Is there anything I should do **4** _____ _____ _____ ?
Contractor:	Make sure you clean the gutters regularly. **5** _____ _____ _____ _____ could still get in there and clog them.
Homeowner:	Okay. **6** _____ _____ _ _____ to do that.

Speaking

8 With a partner, act out the roles below based on Task 7. Then, switch roles.

Student A: You are a contractor. Talk to Student B about:

• repairs done to a roof

• what was causing the leak

• what Student B should do in the future

Student B: You are a homeowner. Talk to Student A about repairs done to a roof.

Writing

9 Use the article and the conversation from Task 8 to write a roof inspection and repair report. Write about:

• leaks found

• repairs done

• maintenance tips

rain

29

14 Roofs 2

mansard roof

ridge

hip

gabled roof

gambrel roof

gable

flat roof

parapet

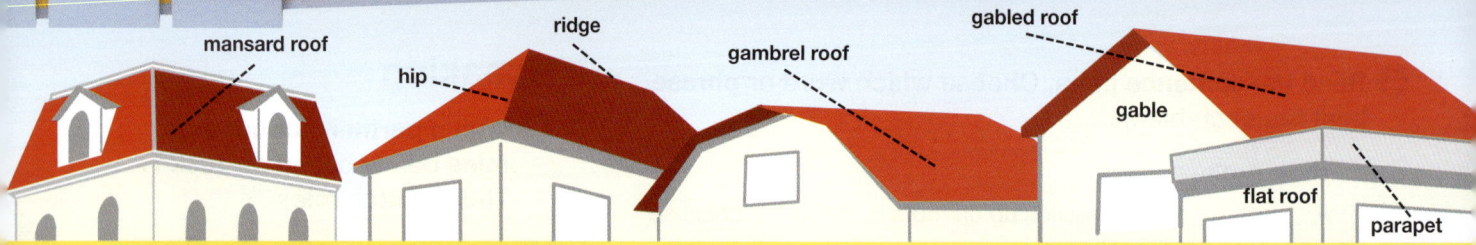

Janet Truman
ROOFING SPECIALIST

shingle

rafter

With over twenty-five years of experience in the roofing industry, I have the skills to make your roofing project a success. I can work with you to design and build the roof of any structure. Need proof? Check out my work around town.

My crew installed the **low slope roof** on the new Super Save store. The **gambrel** roofs of the Anderson and Mayfield farms are my work. And I led the team building the **mansard** roof for the City Living apartment complex.

I can build and design a roof with multiple elements. It could have eye-catching **gables** or slopes that join at **hips**. A simple **shed** roof can have a **rake** or be designed with decorative **eaves** to enhance appearance. Besides looks, I also install functional roofs. Even a **flat roof** will have an effective slope for water drainage.

Additionally, I specialize in the repair of existing roofs. A regular attic inspection to check for damage to **rafters** and **purlins** is always a good idea. My crew and I lay and repair various types of **shingles**, including **shakes**, fiberglass asphalt, and slate. We also check roof **vents** for leaks and proper functioning.

Come to Truman Roofing for a free consultation about your roofing design, installation, or repair needs.

Get ready!

① **Before you read the passage, talk about these questions.**

1 What are some different types of roof?

2 What type of roof has a parapet?

Reading

② **Read the ad for a roof specialist. Then, mark the following statements as true (T) or false (F).**

1 __ The roofer designed mansard roofs for farmhouses.

2 __ Decorative eaves can be added to shed roofs.

3 __ The roofer can repair damaged shakes.

Vocabulary

③ **Match the words (1-7) with the definitions (A-G).**

1 __ shake   4 __ mansard   7 __ rake

2 __ gambrel   5 __ low slope roof

3 __ shed   6 __ purlin

A a kind of roof that has one single slope

B the sloped edge of a roof next to the first or last rafter

C a roof that has a very small slope to allow for water drainage

D a type of wooden shingle made from split logs

E a roof with two slopes on each of each sides, which joins together in hips at the building corners

F a horizontal structural member that connects two roof rafters

G a symmetrical two-sided roof with two slopes on each side

④ **Read the sentences and choose the correct words or phrases.**

1 The column sticking out of the roof is a piping **vent / gable**.

2 The slopes of this mansard roof join in a(n) **eave / hip** at the building corner.

3 This **flat roof / rafter** has a very small slope for water drainage.

4 The **eave / shingle** hangs over the wall for water to run off.

5 The **rafters / vents** supporting this gambrel roof are at two angles.

6 A shed roof does not form a triangle-shaped **rake / gable**.

7 Use asphalt **shingles / purlins** to cover this roof.

5 🎧 Listen and read the ad for a roof specialist again. What type of shingles does the roofer work with?

Listening

6 🎧 Listen to a conversation between an architect and a future homeowner. Choose the correct answers.

1 What is the conversation mainly about?

    A why a gambrel roof is better than a mansard

    B which roof type to install on a new house

    C the difficulties of installing a mansard roof

    D which roofs drain water the best

2 What is a particular advantage of the mansard roof?

    A It is inexpensive to build.

    B It drains water especially well.

    C It provides more space on the top floor.

    D It has two different slopes on each side.

7 🎧 Listen again and complete the conversation.

Architect:	Ah yes. How may I help you today?
Homeowner:	I was thinking about the roof. I'd like to **1** _____ _____ _____ .
Architect:	Certainly. There are several options. For example, **2** _____ _____ _____ roof, you get a symmetrical roof with two different slopes on each side.
Homeowner:	Interesting. **3** _____ _____ _____ of that design?
Architect:	It **4** _____ _____ _____ , but also gives you a lot of headroom on the top floor.
Homeowner:	I see. What are some **5** _____ _____ ?
Architect:	There's also a mansard roof. It's similar to a gambrel, but the **6** _____ _____ _____ at the corners.
Homeowner:	What does that mean, exactly?
Architect:	The slopes come together. A gambrel roof has vertical gables on the ends instead.
Homeowner:	Ah, I understand. Is there an advantage to the mansard design?
Architect:	It makes the most use of the attic and often looks more decorative.

Speaking

8 With a partner, act out the roles below based on Task 7. Then, switch roles.

USE LANGUAGE SUCH AS:

With a ... you get ...

What's the benefit of ...?

Is there an ...

Student A: You are an architect. Talk to Student B about:

• the design for a new roof

• the benefits of different designs

Student B: You are a future homeowner. Talk to Student A about the design for a new roof.

Writing

9 Use the ad and the conversation from Task 8 to write a roofing information brochure. Write about:

• low slope roofs

• shed roofs

• the benefits of each type

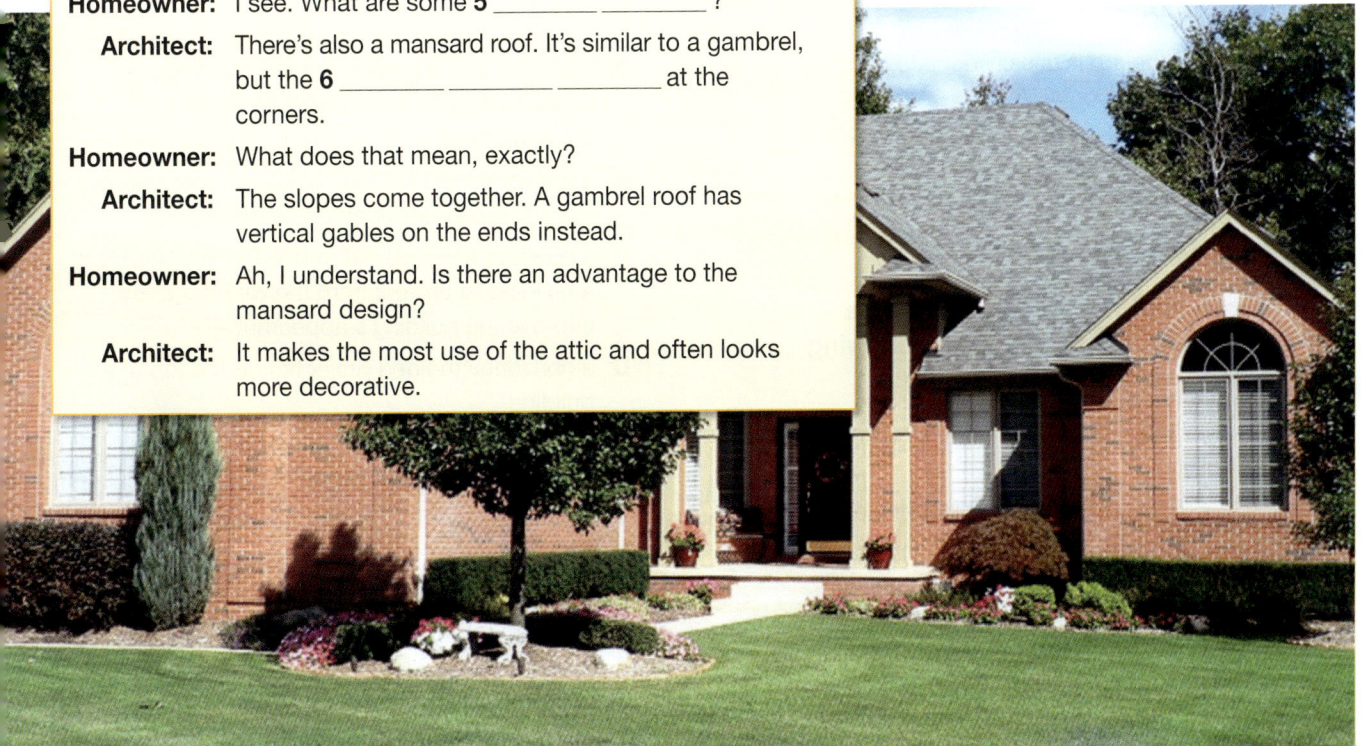

31

siding

cornice

painting

tile

From: Joyce Breyer
To: Dale Reynolds
Re: Finishing Plans

Hi Dale,

Now that the basic design is set, we need to talk about **finishing** your new building.

For **exterior finishing**, what sort of **cladding** would you like? We could go with vinyl **siding**. Masonry provides a more decorative look. A stone **cornice** would look excellent above a brick exterior. That would be more expensive, however.

Several more **interior finishing** details still need to be decided. First, please let us know where to **install partitions** to divide up larger rooms. Then you need to pick out a **painting** scheme for the various interior walls. Two or three similar colors are generally recommended. Also, what sort of **trim** would you like around the doors and windows? Crown molding is very popular for capping, but we can help you design something more unique.

You mentioned earlier that you would like **drop ceilings** in some rooms. Please tell us the exact areas. After they are installed, we can apply a **plaster** coating. Gypsum plaster should be fine for your building's conditions. Last, we know that you want ceramic flooring **tiles**, but you need to choose a design for them.

Please email me the requested information or any questions you have.

Thanks,
Joyce

Get ready!

1 Before you read the passage, talk about these questions.

1 What finishing job is usually done to both outdoor and indoor walls?

2 What kind of floor covering is common in bathrooms?

Reading

2 Read the email from a contractor to a building owner. Then, mark the following statements as true (T) or false (F).

1 __ Vinyl siding is more expensive than masonry cladding.

2 __ Crown molding is used to divide large rooms.

3 __ Drop ceilings are installed after the plaster coating is applied.

Vocabulary

3 Match the words (1-7) with the definitions (A-G).

1 __ cladding   4 __ cornice   7 __ install
2 __ plaster   5 __ finish
3 __ trim   6 __ tile

A a kind of molding used around openings on interior and exterior walls to add details or cover up gaps

B a regular-shaped piece of clay or other material used to cover or decorate a surface

C a construction material applied to the outside of a building to protect from the weather and improve the building's appearance

D a horizontal molded projection at the top of a building

E to set something up or prepare it for use

F to add final parts to a building's interior and exterior once it is structurally complete

G a mixture of dry material and water used to coat walls and ceilings

4 Read the sentence pairs. Choose which word or phrase best fits each blank.

1 exterior finishing / interior finishing

  A The _____ for this building will include landscaping and a parking lot.

  B Cabinets will be installed during the _____ process.

2 siding / painting

  A The owner wants bright colors for both the interior and exterior _____ .

  B Vinyl _____ resists damage from hail.

3 partition / drop ceiling

  A This _____ can be rotracted to make the room larger.

  B What kind of wiring is above this _____ ?

5 🎧 Listen and read the email from a contractor to an owner again. What are some interior finishing decisions that need to be made?

Listening

6 🎧 Listen to a conversation between a contractor and a building owner. Choose the correct answers.

1 What is the conversation mainly about?

  A instructions for interior finishing

  B which exterior cladding to choose

  C when to begin the finishing process

  D errors in an email on finishing choices

2 What is the advantage of vinyl siding?

  A It provides insulation.

  B It lasts longer than masonry.

  C It gives a classic appearance.

  D It is resistant to hail damage.

7 🎧 Listen again and complete the conversation.

Owner:	Well, I've decided on just about everything. I'm just having trouble choosing an **1** _____ _____ .
Contractor:	I see. Maybe I can help you out. **2** _____ _____ are you considering?
Owner:	I want either **3** _____ _____ or a masonry finish.
Contractor:	Those are very different materials, **4** _____ _____ _____ _____ , vinyl siding will give your building a modern look. It's resistant to hail, but doesn't **5** _____ _____ .
Owner:	Okay. What about masonry?
Contractor:	That will give your building a classic look. It will last a long time, unless it's **6** _____ _____ _____ .

Speaking

8 With a partner, act out the roles below based on Task 7. Then, switch roles.

USE LANGUAGE SUCH AS:

I want either ...

On the one hand ...

... will give your building ...

Student A: You are a building owner. Talk to Student B about:

• finishing plans for a building

• options for a finishing plan

• benefits and drawbacks of each option

Student B: You are a contractor. Talk to Student A about finishing plans for a building.

Writing

9 Use the email and the conversation from Task 8 to write an information brochure on exterior cladding. Write about:

• appearance

• benefits

• drawbacks

Glossary

aggregate [N-UNCOUNT-U3] Aggregate is a material that helps bind cement particles together.

air content test [N-COUNT-U4] An air content test is a test for the presence of air in a concrete mix.

air entrainment [N-UNCOUNT-U3] Air entrainment is the process of mixing small air bubbles into concrete.

anchor bolt [N-COUNT-U7] An anchor bolt is a strong bolt used to attach a steel frame to a concrete foundation.

architect's scale [N-COUNT-U2] An architect's scale is an instrument used to measure the scale of construction drawings.

asbestos [N-UNCOUNT-U10] Asbestos is a material that was once widely used as building insulation, but is no longer used due to its potential to cause health problems.

ASTM designation [N-COUNT-U7] An ASTM designation is the strength rating of a structural steel bolt, as assigned by the American Society of Testing and Materials.

automatic door [N-COUNT-U9] An automatic door is a door powered by electricity that opens on its own upon detection of motion or pressure.

awning [N-COUNT-U9] An awning is a window attached to its frame by one or more hinges at its top and swings outward.

baluster [N-COUNT-U11] A baluster is one of the short columns that support a rail on the side of a staircase.

balustrade [N-COUNT-U11] A balustrade is a row of columns topped by a rail on the side of a staircase.

banister [N-COUNT-U11] A banister is the handrail of a staircase.

batt [N-COUNT-U10] A batt is a precut section of rigid panel insulation that fits into a wall cavity.

bearing plate [N-COUNT-U7] A bearing plate is a steel plate with holes to receive anchor bolts, used in steel frame construction.

bearing wall [N-COUNT-U12] A bearing wall is a wall that bears the weight of a load resting on it down to a foundation structure.

bearing-type connection [N-COUNT-U7] A bearing-type connection is a structural steel connection that uses the bolt to transfer load from one piece of steel to another.

belt conveyor [N-COUNT-U5] A belt conveyor is a machine for transporting concrete or other material that consists of two pulleys and a continuous loop of material (such as rubber) that rotates around them.

bifold door [N-COUNT-U9] A bifold door is a door with several sections that fold into pairs, often used as a closet door.

bind [V-T-U3] To bind something is to attach it to something else.

bolting [N-UNCOUNT-U7] Bolting is the use of strong cylindrical metal fasteners to join pieces of a steel frame.

brittle [ADJ-U8] If something is brittle, it breaks or snaps easily when pressure is applied.

bucket [N-COUNT-U5] A bucket is a cylindrical container used to transport concrete or other materials, often lifted by a crane.

buggy [N-COUNT-U5] A buggy is a small man-powered or motorized vehicle used to transport materials at a construction site.

building envelope [N-COUNT-U10] A building envelope is the part of the building that separates the inside from the outside, including walls, doors, and windows.

casement [N-COUNT-U9] A casement is a window attached to its frame by one or more hinges at its side.

cavity wall [N-COUNT-U12] A cavity wall is a wall that has two skins made from brick or concrete that are separated by a hollow space.

cement paste [N-UNCOUNT-U3] Cement paste is the paste formed when water and cement are combined.

centerline [N-COUNT-U2] A centerline is a line in a drawing that shows the center axis of an object.

chute [N-COUNT-U5] A chute is a long tube or trough through which concrete or other material can travel from a higher level to a lower level.

cladding [N-UNCOUNT-U15] Cladding is a construction material applied to the outside of a building to protect it from the weather and improve the building's appearance.

cleanliness [N-UNCOUNT-U4] Cleanliness is a measurement of the presence of silt and other matter sticking to coarse aggregates used in a concrete mix.

coarse aggregate [N-COUNT-U3] A coarse aggregate is an aggregate made from a coarse material, like gravel.

collapse [N-UNCOUNT-U4] Collapse is a kind of a concrete slump in which the concrete collapses completely, usually indicating a mix that is too wet.

colorimetric test [N-COUNT-U4] A colorimetric test is a test to determine the presence of fine organic matter in fine aggregate.

column [N-COUNT-U7] A column is the primary vertical piece of a steel frame.

complex [ADJ-U1] If an object is complex, it is made up of many parts or very detailed.

concrete [N-UNCOUNT-U3] Concrete is a mixture of cement, water, and aggregates.

concrete frame [N-COUNT-U8] A concrete frame is a structural building frame made of concrete and reinforced by steel.

cornice [N-COUNT-U15] A cornice is a horizontal molded projection at the top of a building.

countercurrent mixer [N-COUNT-U5] A countercurrent mixer is a concrete mixer that consists of a large pan that rotates in a clockwise direction and three mixing tools that rotate in a counterclockwise direction.

coupler [N-COUNT-U8] A coupler is a device used to splice pieces of reinforced steel consisting of two female ends.

cover [N-UNCOUNT-U8] A cover is something that is placed over something else in order to hide or protect it.

cross section [N-COUNT-U1] A cross section is the point where a two-dimensional plane intersects with a three-dimensional object, as shown in a section drawing.

curtain wall [N-COUNT-U12] A curtain wall is a wall that is non-structural and only serves to keep out the weather.

cutting-plane line [N-COUNT-U2] A cutting-plane line is a line in a drawing that indicates where a section view is taken from and in what direction it is viewed.

dead load [N-COUNT-U6] A dead load is a force on a building structure that does not change over time, such as that of the building itself and permanent fixtures.

deflection [N-UNCOUNT-U6] Deflection is a measure of how much a piece of timber changes shape under the pressure of a load.

dimension line [N-COUNT-U2] A dimension line is a line in a drawing that shows the size (such as length or width) of an object.

double-hung [ADJ-U9] If a window is double-hung, it has two parts, or sashes, that overlap slightly and slide up and down inside its frame.

drain [N-COUNT-U13] A drain is an opening that allows liquid to flow out of a space.

drop ceiling [N-COUNT-U15] A drop ceiling is a second ceiling suspended from above that conceals wiring, plumbing, and venting ducts.

drum mixer [N-COUNT-U5] A drum mixer is a concrete mixer that consists of a rotating drum with stationary blades inside.

eave [N-COUNT-U14] An eave is the lower edge of a building's roof, which usually extends beyond the building's wall to carry rainwater away.

elements [N-PLURAL-U13] The elements are various types of weather, such as wind, snow, or rain.

Glossary

elevation [N-COUNT-U1] An elevation is a view of something from the side, showing its height.

erection mark [N-COUNT-U7] An erection mark is a mark on a piece of steel frame that shows where it goes in the frame.

extension line [N-COUNT-U2] An extension line is a line in a drawing that shows the extent of a dimension line.

exterior finishing [N-UNCOUNT-U15] Exterior finishing is the final additions to the outside of a building, such as cladding, windows, and landscaping.

fillet weld [N-COUNT-U7] A fillet weld is a type of welding used in steel frame construction that does not require preparation of the material that is welded.

fine aggregate [N-COUNT-U3] A fine aggregate is an aggregate made from a fine material, like sand.

finish [V-T-U5] To finish concrete is to alter concrete surfaces to produce the desired final appearance and texture.

finish [V-T-U15] To finish a building is to add final parts to its interior and exterior once it is structurally complete.

fire door [N-COUNT-U9] A fire door is a door with a high fire resistance rating used as part of a building's fire protection system.

fixed [ADJ-U9] If a window is fixed, it cannot be opened.

flashing [N-COUNT-U13] A flashing is a roof component used to seal roof edges where the roof covering is interrupted.

flat roof [N-COUNT-U14] A flat roof is a roof that appears flat but has a very small slope to allow for water drainage.

flight [N-COUNT-U11] A flight of stairs is one set of steps from one floor to the next.

float [N-COUNT-U5] A float is a rectangular tool used to smooth and level the top layer of concrete.

frame sash [N-COUNT-U9] A frame sash is a movable panel in a window that holds panes of glass.

friction-type connection [N-COUNT-U7] A friction-type connection is a structural steel connection that uses the friction between connected surfaces to transfer load from one piece to another.

gable [N-COUNT-U14] A gable is the triangular portion of a roof between the sloping edges.

gambrel [N-COUNT-U14] A gambrel is a symmetrical two-sided roof with two slopes on each side.

gauge [N-COUNT-U7] A gauge is the distance between a row of bolts in a steel frame connection.

girder [N-COUNT-U7] A girder is the primary horizontal piece of a steel frame.

glass wool blanket [N-COUNT-U10] A glass wool blanket is a piece of fiberglass insulation that is sold in a continuous roll.

glued-laminated timber [N-UNCOUNT-U6] Glued-laminated timber is a timber product that has several layers of timber glued together with strong adhesive.

glulam rivet [N-COUNT-U6] A glulam rivet is a special steel nail used in connections of glued-laminated timber.

going [N-UNCOUNT-U11] Going is the distance from the edge of a nosing to the edge of nosing in plan view.

gradation [N-UNCOUNT-U4] Gradation is the distribution of particle sizes in the aggregate used in a concrete mix.

gravel stop [N-COUNT-U13] A gravel stop is a piece of metal placed at the edge of a roof to prevent gravel from falling off.

groove weld [N-COUNT-U7] A groove weld is a type of welding used in steel frame construction that joins pieces of metal that are at 90 degree angles.

grout [N-UNCOUNT-U12] Grout is a construction material composed of water, cement, and sand that is used to embed rebars in masonry walls, fill voids, and seal joints.

gutter [N-COUNT-U13] A gutter is a channel at the edge of a roof that collects rainwater and carries it away.

heavyweight concrete [N-UNCOUNT-U3] Heavyweight concrete is a type of concrete that has a density of 189 to 380 lb/cu ft.

hidden line [N-COUNT-U2] A hidden line is a line in a drawing that shows edges that are hidden from normal view.

hip [N-COUNT-U14] A hip is the edge where two sloping surfaces of a roof join.

hopper [N-COUNT-U9] A hopper is a window attached to its frame by one or more hinges at the bottom.

horizontally [ADV-U1] If a line is drawn horizontally, it is drawn straight from left to right.

install [V-T-U15] To install something is to set it up or prepare it for use.

insulating concrete [N-UNCOUNT-U3] Insulating concrete is a type of non-structural concrete that has a density of 15 to 90 lb/cu ft.

insulating concrete form [N-UNCOUNT-U10] Insulating concrete form is a stay-in-place formwork that provides permanent building insulation, made of an insulating material and filled with concrete.

insulation [N-UNCOUNT-U10] Insulation is material in a building's walls that reduces the flow of heat into or out of the building.

interior finishing [N-UNCOUNT-U15] Interior finishing is the adding of final features to the inside of a building, such as partitions, stairs, and fixtures.

irregular [ADJ-U1] If a shape is irregular, it does not have many straight lines.

isometric drawing [N-COUNT-U1] An isometric drawing is a construction drawing with objects shown in three dimensions by drawing horizontal lines at a 30 degree angle.

landing [N-COUNT-U11] A landing is a platform at the bottom, at the top, or in between sets of stairs.

lap splice [N-COUNT-U8] A lap splice is a method of splicing reinforcing steel in which the ends of each member overlap each other.

leader [N-COUNT-U2] A leader is a line in a drawing that connects an object with its label.

lightweight concrete [N-UNCOUNT-U3] Lightweight concrete is a type of concrete that has a density of 85 to 115 lb/cu ft.

live load [N-COUNT-U6] A live load is a temporary or moving force on a structure, such as vehicles travelling over a bridge.

loose fill [N-UNCOUNT-U10] Loose fill is a type of insulation that does not have a solid form and therefore can be blown or sprayed into small spaces.

low slope roof [N-COUNT-U14] A low slope roof is a roof that has a small slope to allow for water drainage.

mansard [N-COUNT-U14] A mansard is a roof with two slopes on each of each sides, which joins together in hips at the building corners.

mason [N-COUNT-U12] A mason is a person who builds structures with stone or brick.

masonry [N-UNCOUNT-U12] Masonry is the building of a structure from individual pieces of brick, concrete, or another material, joined together by mortar.

masonry unit [N-COUNT-U12] A masonry unit is a single piece of masonry, such as a concrete brick.

mechanical splice [N-COUNT-U8] A mechanical splice is a method of splicing reinforcing steel consisting of a metal sleeve held in place by a wedge driven over the sleeve ends.

member [N-COUNT-U7] A member is an individual piece of a structural frame, made of steel, timber, or concrete.

mixing [N-UNCOUNT-U5] Mixing is the process of combining and stirring cement, water, and aggregate until it forms a concrete mix.

moisture test [N-COUNT-U4] A moisture test is a test for the presence and level of water in an aggregate.

Glossary

mortar [N-UNCOUNT-U12] Mortar is paste used in construction to bind construction blocks together and seal gaps between them.

multiwythe [ADJ-U12] If a wall is multiwythe, it has a thickness of two or more blocks.

natural fiber [N-UNCOUNT-U10] Natural fiber is a material used as building insulation that is found in nature rather than manmade, such as cork, cotton, or wool.

newel [N-COUNT-U11] A newel is a sturdy pillar at the top or bottom of a staircase, which supports the banister.

normal-weight concrete [N-UNCOUNT-U3] Normal-weight concrete is a type of concrete that has a density of 135 to 160 lb/cu ft.

nosing [N-COUNT-U11] A nosing is the part of a tread of a step that projects over the riser underneath it.

object line [N-COUNT-U2] An object line is a solid line in a drawing that shows the shape of an object.

oblique drawing [N-COUNT-U1] An oblique drawing is a drawing that shows one surface of an object on the plane of the paper and the adjacent surface at an angle.

open-web steel joist [N-COUNT-U7] An open-web steel joist is a lightweight truss used to support a roof or floor in steel frame construction.

organic impurity [N-COUNT-U4] An organic impurity is the presence of fine organic material in a concrete aggregate, possibly making it unfit for use.

orthographic projection [N-COUNT-U1] An orthographic projection is a type of drawing that separates each side of an object and shows it flat, as if projected against the side of a glass box.

painting [N-UNCOUNT-U15] Painting is the application of paint to a building's interior or exterior walls to improve their appearance and protect them from damage.

pane [N-COUNT-U9] A pane is a section of glass in a window surrounded by a frame.

parapet [N-COUNT-U13] A parapet is a part of a building's edge, such as a wall, that extends above the roof.

partition [N-COUNT-U15] A partition is a vertical structure that divides a room.

pin-type connection [N-COUNT-U6] A pin-type connection is a timber connector that uses thin plates and bolts to join timber pieces and which allows for some rotation between the pieces.

pitch [N-COUNT-U7] A pitch is the distance between the center of holes in a row of bolts in a steel frame connection.

place [V-T-U5] To place concrete is to put it in its final position.

plan view [N-COUNT-U1] A plan view, also known as a bird's-eye view, is a construction drawing shown from above.

plaster [N-UNCOUNT-U15] Plaster is a mixture of dry material and water used to coat walls and ceilings.

pocket door [N-COUNT-U9] A pocket door is a sliding door that, when opened, moves completely inside a compartment in the wall next to it.

precast [ADJ-U8] If a concrete member is precast, it is formed and cured at a plant and brought to the building site.

prestressed [ADJ-U8] If concrete is prestressed, it has had tendons added and tightened to overcome its weakness in tension.

purlin [N-COUNT-U14] A purlin is a horizontal structural member that connects two roof rafters.

R-value [N-COUNT-U10] An R-value is a rating of an insulation material's effectiveness.

rafter [N-COUNT-U14] A rafter is a sloping structural member that supports the roof of a building.

rain [N-UNCOUNT-U13] Rain is water that falls from a cloud.

rake [N-COUNT-U14] A rake is the sloped edge of a roof next to the first or last rafter.

reinforcement [N-COUNT-U8] A reinforcement is something that is added to something else to make it stronger.

revolving door [N-COUNT-U9] A **revolving door** is a door with three or four separate doors that attach to a center shaft and rotate within an enclosed space.

rigid panel [N-COUNT-U10] A **rigid panel** is a kind of building insulation made from fibrous materials or plastic foam, often sold in sections.

riser [N-COUNT-U11] A **riser** is the vertical part of a step.

riser height [N-UNCOUNT-U11] **Riser height** is the vertical distance of a riser in a set of stairs.

roof [N-COUNT-U13] A **roof** is the cover at the top of a building.

roof deck [N-COUNT-U13] A **roof deck** is a layer of roofing material in between the structural parts and insulating or waterproofing layers.

roof frame [N-COUNT-U13] A **roof frame** is the structural support of a roof of a building.

roof membrane [N-COUNT-U13] A **roof membrane** is a layer of rubber or bitumen placed typically over a flat roof to prevent water leakage.

scale [N-UNCOUNT-U2] **Scale** is the relationship between the size of a plan or drawing and the actual object or structure it represents.

scale drawing [N-COUNT-U2] A **scale drawing** is a drawing of a construction project that shows everything proportionately smaller than it really is.

screed [N-COUNT-U5] A **screed** is a tool used to level a layer of material, such as cement.

scupper [N-COUNT-U13] A **scupper** is an opening in a wall that allows water to drain off of a roof.

section [N-COUNT-U1] A **section** is a view of an object's middle, as if it had been cut in half.

section shape [N-COUNT-U7] A **section shape** is the specific shape of a piece of structural steel.

set [V-I-U3] To **set** is to become hard and solid.

shake [N-COUNT-U14] A **shake** is a type of wooden shingle made from split logs.

shear [N-UNCOUNT-U4] **Shear** is a kind of concrete slump in which the top portion of the concrete breaks off and slips sideways.

shear plate [N-COUNT-U6] A **shear plate** is a device that distributes force over a large area of timber in order to prevent damage.

shed [N-COUNT-U14] A **shed** is a kind of roof that has one single slope.

shingle [N-COUNT-U14] A **shingle** is a thin piece of building material laid in rows as a roof covering.

shrink [V-I-U3] To **shrink** is to become smaller.

siding [N-UNCOUNT-U15] **Siding** is an outer covering of a building made from boards of wood, plastic, asphalt, or metal, which protects the building from weather effects.

silt test [N-COUNT-U4] A **silt test** is a test to determine the presence of very fine material in a coarse aggregate.

single wythe [ADJ-U12] If a wall is **single wythe**, it has a thickness of one block.

sketch [N-COUNT-U1] A **sketch** is a quickly drawn picture that only shows the main details or outlines.

sliding [ADJ-U9] If a door or window is **sliding**, it opens by moving horizontally.

slope [N-COUNT-U13] A **slope** is the diagonal angle of a roof.

slump test [N-COUNT-U4] A **slump test** is a test to measure the flowability of a concrete mix.

snow [N-UNCOUNT-U13] **Snow** is frozen crystals of water that fall from a cloud.

soundness [N-UNCOUNT-U4] **Soundness** is a measurement of the strength of an aggregate used in a concrete mix.

spandrel [N-COUNT-U11] A **spandrel** is the triangular space underneath a set of stairs.

Glossary

specific gravity [N-UNCOUNT-U4] Specific gravity is the ratio of something's mass to the mass of an equal volume of water.

splice [V-T-U8] To splice pieces of reinforcing steel is to join them together permanently.

split-ring connector [N-COUNT-U6] A split-ring connector is a timber connector that transfers a load through a ring instead of a bolt.

spray polyurethane foam (SPF) [N-UNCOUNT-U10] Spray polyurethane foam is a type of building insulation that is sprayed from a gun and expands into spaces in walls.

stairs [N-UNCOUNT-U11] Stairs are steps that connect two floors in a building.

steel frame [N-COUNT-U7] A steel frame is a building frame made of steel components, which can support a building many stories tall.

strike off [V-T-U5] To strike off finished concrete is to use a screed to level it off and remove excess material.

stringer [N-COUNT-U11] A stringer is the structural part of a staircase that supports the risers and treads.

tensile strength [N-UNCOUNT-U8] Tensile strength is the maximum amount of stress that a material can withstand while being stretched before damage occurs to its cross-section.

tile [N-COUNT-U15] A tile is a regular-shaped piece of clay or other material used to cover or decorate a surface.

timber [N-UNCOUNT-U6] Timber is precut wood that is ready to be used in construction.

timber connectors [N-COUNT-U6] Timber connectors are devices using bolts and other steel pieces that join one piece of a timber frame to another and anchor the frame to its foundation.

transfer [V-T-U6] To transfer a load is to move its weight to a different load-bearing structure.

tread [N-COUNT-U11] A tread is the horizontal part of a step.

tread depth [N-UNCOUNT-U11] Tread depth is the horizontal distance of a tread in a set of stairs.

trim [N-UNCOUNT-U15] Trim is a kind of molding used around openings on interior and exterior walls to add details or cover up gaps.

trowel [N-COUNT-U5] A trowel is a steel tool used to produce a smooth concrete surface.

true slump [N-UNCOUNT-U4] True slump is a concrete slump in which the concrete more or less keeps its shape.

truss plate [N-COUNT-U6] A truss plate is a metal plate used to connect timber of the same thickness in the same plane.

uniformity [N-UNCOUNT-U5] Uniformity is the state of being the same or alike throughout.

vapor barrier [N-COUNT-U13] A vapor barrier is material that prevents moisture from entering a wall, roof, or floor.

vapor retarder [N-COUNT-U10] A vapor retarder is a material that resists penetration by moisture, placed in building walls, floors, and ceilings.

veneer [N-UNCOUNT-U12] Veneer is a wall that has one masonry layer backed by an airspace.

vent [N-COUNT-U14] A vent is a pipe or duct that extends through a roof to convey exhaust gases.

vertically [ADV-U1] If a line is drawn vertically, it is drawn straight up and down.

void [N-COUNT-U3] A void is a gap.

walk [N-COUNT-U13] A walk is a place along a roof in which it is possible to walk.

water:cement ratio [N-UNCOUNT-U4] Water:cement ratio is the amount of water used per unit of cement in a concrete mix.

welded splice [N-COUNT-U8] A welded splice is a method of splicing reinforcing steel that welds the pieces together.

welded wire reinforcement [N-UNCOUNT-U8] Welded wire reinforcement is a method of reinforcing concrete using wire rods welded into grids.